MIRACLES & MEMORIES

MIRACLES & MEMORIES

Gertrude Brown

iUniverse, Inc.
New York Lincoln Shanghai

Miracles & Memories

iUniverse books may be ordered through booksellers or by contacting:

iUniverse
2021 Pine Lake Road, Suite 100
Lincoln, NE 68512
www.iuniverse.com
1-800-Authors (1-800-288-4677)

Because of the dynamic nature of the Internet, any Web addresses or links contained in this book may have changed since publication and may no longer be valid.

The views expressed in this work are solely those of the author and do not necessarily reflect the views of the publisher, and the publisher hereby disclaims any responsibility for them.

ISBN: 978-0-595-47056-3 (pbk)
ISBN: 978-0-595-91338-1 (ebk)

Printed in the United States of America

C O N T E N T S

ACKNOWLEDGEMENTS

Thanks to all who encouraged me to write this "Book." To my husband Bobby who motivated me to write for years. He also brought about much laughter when he reminded me of things that I mention in our short stories. He has inspired me in many ways. And was truly an angel during my sickness.

To my children, Steve and Randy for reminding me of some of the memories of their childhood and to Steve for helping so much in the computer work, and for compiling the family photos. I could not have done it alone.

For my favorite former pastors that obeyed God and came to pray for us in my special time of need.

To Rev. Melvin Charles and Sandra

Rev. Jesse Ogden and Patricia

Rev. Curtis Scott and family

To my Doctors: Dr. Roseanne Weaver, who encouraged me to get one more test when I was ready to give up.

Dr. Mark Vrana, who was honest in his valuation, and did everything he could to help me.

Dr. Beltran, who encouraged me to write a book about my healing,

And all prayers of family members, friends and people I did not know.

And to God, who answered prayers and gave me a supernatural Healing "TO HIM BE THE GLORY!"

INTRODUCTION

This book is written in four parts:

Part 1: Supernatural Healing.

Part 2: Memories of my childhood from 1933 and our family lives in short stories that will make you laugh, and perhaps shed some tears.

Part 3: Memories of Bobby's childhood from 1930 in North Georgia and their family lives in short stories.

Part 4: Photo Scrap Book

Our intentions are to open up our lives before you, the good and the not so good, and to encourage the readers that hard times can be stepping stones to a better life. Lives in Georgia during the depression years were especially hard on the working class of people with large families. But trusting God and living a determined life will change poverty into plenty.

PART 1:

"SUPERNATURAL HEALING"

"TRAGEDY STRIKES"

Christmas had come and gone in 1993. Our family had met at our house for our Christmas Eve get together and we all had a wonderful time. Now it was time to get back to work. At our mattress factory we were busy getting ready for the coming year. We had new carpet installed in our showroom and more room in the work area and storage area made during the time the employees had off. Now orders were being filled and shipments were going out. But this came to a sudden halt, when the heat furnace exploded on the 18th of January. Everything was completely destroyed quickly by fire. Needless to say the rest of the year was not a time of rejoicing. It was a very stressful year for Bobby and me. To complete the un-finished jobs, Bobby and his assistant set up shop in our garage. He would not think of letting un-finished business stop him.

"1994 LOOKING GOOD"

Bobby and I had our yearly physicals as usual. All lab tests made us think we were in very good condition. And since our insurance premiums were so high, we decided to just cancel our hospitalization insurance and save our money. Since money was going out, but none coming in. That was a terrible mistake because in just a few months, it seemed that my body was falling apart. At this time, looking good was not in my vocabulary. Instead of feeling good, I was feeling terrible. I knew something really bad was happening. I had an infection that my doctor could not cure with antibiotics, so she sent me to a kidney specialist. I wasn't at an "Amusement Park" but I was on a merry go round, that didn't seem to stop. I was sent from one doctor to another, test after test. I had Ultrasounds, X-rays, Plylograms, Ekg's. Stress test, Cat scans, Upper GI's, Cystoscope, Colonoscopy, Chest x-ray, Mammograms and none of these revealed anything unusual. I had started on a journey I had not planned on. It was like I was put on a bumpy train with a ticket to "destination" un-known.

"NIGHTS SEEMED LIKE ETERNITY"

I was having heart burn so bad, I could not lie in the bed. My recliner chair became my bed. We started buying "TUMS" in large jars. But they didn't help much. I would curl up in the chair for very long nights. Living in the country in '94 there was no traffic on the road at night. I would yearn to hear a car come by, because I knew that would be the men that worked at a near by dairy, and daybreak was close. It even seemed like God had taken a vacation. My calendar was so full of doctor appointments. I was going about every two weeks, and most of the visits were followed with a visit to a hospital for more test. My side hurt all the time, and I couldn't eat the things I always liked the most. Holidays were coming up, and the turkey and dressing, cakes and candy could not be tolerated. Bobby and I had been Christians for a long time, and we believed in healing and the power of prayer. But now the only way I could describe my situation was "suffering." But I remembered what Paul said in Romans 8:18. "I reckon the sufferings of this present time are not worthy to be compared with the glory which shall be revealed in us."

"YOU HAVE GALLSTONES"

What doctor do you want to have for the surgery? Well, I wasn't expecting that. But I replied I don't know any surgeons here, and an appointment was made for me. That trip to the doctor called for another hospital test, which concluded there were no gallstones. I never got an answer for the pain in my side. I was still doing my light house work, but I tired easily and was loosing lots of weight too. Then another un-expected problem showed up. I started burning under my arm and in just a few minutes, a big lump came up. That was a startling thing to happen. And it happened on Friday, and I waited until Monday to see my doctor. She wanted me to see a doctor in Athens right away, and made an appointment for me. A faithful minister that we knew, Rev. Curtis Scott wanted to go with us to the hospital and at 5 o'clock that morning he was ready to go. We appreciated his faithfulness so much. That lump called for an operation. But after two labs examined the results, it was not cancer as they both had supposed. After that I had to have two mammograms before they would release me. They saw no problem with those. Another miracle had happened.

"CONVERSATION BETWEEN GOD AND JOB"

Just what did Job and God talk about? I re-read the scriptures. God told Satan that Job was a perfect and upright man and he feared God, but Satan realized God had a hedge around him and said, if you will remove that hedge, he will curse you to your face. My problems were not equal to Job's, but I felt like they were getting pretty close. I have learned before there's a victory, there's always a battle. Thank God for the hedge he has around his believers. John 9:31 says "If any man is a worshipper of God, and doeth his will, him he heareth." To my knowledge, I have always wanted to do God's will. Bobby and I were born again a year after our marriage at a tent revival. It was a different kind of service. I was not familiar with going to a meeting that was Pentecostal in faith. But my eyes were opened, and my heart was stirred. We went up front and knelt at a bench that was set up as the altar. Wood shavings covered the ground, and we both accepted Jesus as our Saviour, and from then on, we were new creatures, and loved to attend and work in churches. Our vacations were always planned so we could be back in church on Sunday. So I believed that scripture was for me too.

"A LIVER BIOPSY"

By this time I was being told my liver had enlarged. My local doctor insisted I see a liver doctor. I was so sick and tired of seeing doctors and having test, I just refused to go to another one. Now, I really appreciated her telling me that my liver was so enlarged, that it was sagging below my waistline, and I must go right away. So off I went. This doctor wanted to delete all my records and start from the beginning and do all of the tests again. That I flatly refused. I knew my body could not stand that again, so I came back and went to a liver doctor in Athens. I let him do a liver biopsy, even though I knew it was dangerous since it was so enlarged. But what did I have to loose? Philippians 1:20 Paul said Christ shall be magnified in my body. Weather it is by life or death, but for me to live is Christ and to die is gain. I had lost over 40 lbs. and had no strength left. When the report came back the diagnosis was, you have "amyloidosis" in your liver. This sounded better than cancer, even though I didn't know what it did mean. Then my next appointment was with an oncologist. I wondered why. I was told then that amyloidosis was very rare, only a few cases in the US. He also wanted to do a bone marrow test, because cancer and amyloidosis usually follows each other. On my next trip, I was told something that was dreadful to hear. You have cancer cells in your bone marrow. Then he said both are very aggressive, and not a cure for either. I didn't show any emotion, since I had been so sick and worn out I really didn't care, but I had my family to think about. There is a stigmatism almost like leprosy about the word cancer. You feel shameful and almost un-clean. The cancer cells "multiple myeloma" was in my bone marrow.

On the way home we sat quietly, and Bobby kept encouraging me saying we will beat this thing, you will be alright. Now this was the seventh specialist I had been to. What a blessed person I am to have a husband that's so faithful and loving to me.

"CHEMO TREATMENTS"

The next trip, I was started on Chemo pills, with steroids. I had never been as sick before as I was that night. After two treatments, he warned me about some symptoms that might occur. And if these happen you must get to a hospital quickly. A high fever, chills, and sore throat were some of them. By this time, my body was a total wreck. Not one part of my body functioned properly. I was told that amyloid was all over my body. The nerve itch was caused from my nerve endings being coated with the amyloid. Some scriptures kept coming to my mind about the bone marrow. Proverbs 3:5–9 was the one. "Trust in the Lord with all your heart, and lean not unto thine own understanding. In all your ways acknowledge him, and he shall direct your paths. Be not wise in your own eyes, fear the Lord, and depart from evil." And this is the verse that really hit me. "It shall be health to thy navel (body) and marrow to thy bones."That was the one I was looking for! I am so glad that I had learned promises of God earlier before I got sick. Because at this time I was not able to hold a Bible, neither could I concentrate on new verses, but there's power and healing in the Word.

"YOU HAVE 3 MONTHS OR LESS TO LIVE"

Back in his office on Sept.1, 1995 the doctor brought his veri-fied facts on paper. He knew there was no way I could live. He was very stern and honest, and said Mrs. Brown, the things I have done have not helped at all. I don't see any need of making you any sicker than you are. Your immune system is so low you can't resist any sickness,you are at high risk of a coronary heart attack, and your liver has caused your cholesterol to build up. I just listened, not saying a word. He couldn't understand how I was taking this message so lightly. Then the punch line came. "You have 3 months or less to live." I saw a tear in Bobby's eye, and if it had not been for him and the family, I would have wel-comed death. Our boys and their families were home waiting for a report from us. That's when it really got bad. They were going to a school ball game in Hazlehurst, and would spend the week-end. That's when we both got speechless. I looked at Bobby and even he could not talk now. Finally the family was told and after the crying and talking was over, Steve sat beside me and took my hand. He prayed a prayer of scripture prom-ises. He asked me to agree with him on "Matthew 18:19 Again I say unto you that if two of you shall agree on earth as touching any thing that they shall ask it shall be done for them by my father who is in Heaven." We agreed and many times when I would have liked to give up, I would remember the agreement and prayers of my family. Randy was deeply hurt, but he, being a lots like me could not express him self. No worldly riches can compare with a family that prays.

"FACTS VERSUS TRUTH"

Now it's down to the wire. Do you believe the Truth or Facts? Facts said I couldn't live, but Truth said, "By his stripes you were healed." I really believe if you can hold to the truth long enough, it will change the facts. But do believe me when I say Satan does not give up easy. The faith walk is not easy, but is a "Must" Proverbs 4:20–22 says my son, attend to my words; incline thine ear unto my sayings. Let them "not" depart from thine eyes; keep them in the midst of thine heart. For they are life unto those that find them, and "health" to all their flesh. That reminds me of what Abraham did. He called the things that were not as though they were. He was a good example for us. I must not dwell on the sickness, but keep looking and expecting health. And Bobby's words, we will make it!

"SYMPTOMS APPEAR"

Sept 1995, looking like it would be a good day. Bobby was bringing breakfast to the bedroom now, since I did not feel like walking to the kitchen. This day, he had brought my breakfast which he had cooked. He was a very good cook, and planner. He always insisted on me eating a good meal every time. But this day, things turned. I started having the symptoms that had been described to me, chills and fever set in. Then my muscles started giving away. The doctor was called and I slid my feet to the floor to walk. But I could not pick them up. Randy picked me up and carried me to the car. The doctor immediately had me enrolled in the hospital and started testing me, which lasted all night. I was asked what kind of medicine I was taking but I could not tell them. I said you will just have to look at my records. The next day, Bobby left just long enough to get more clothes, and tend to some things at home, and a previous pastor, Melvin Charles had heard about my sickness, but had no idea I was in the hospital. Another miracle happened. Just as Bobby was coming out of our driveway, Melvin drove up. He had come from Savannah, Georgia and the two met. That reminded me of when Jesus sent Peter and John to go and prepare the Passover. Luke 22:10 says follow the man with a pitcher of water. Suppose the man had been detained and was not there with the water? Suppose Peter and John decided to stop on the way. The meeting could not have happened. They would not have found the furnished room for the Passover. These meetings must be ordained by God! Melvin, I believe had been sent by God. He came on to the hospital, talked a short time and had prayer and left. He reminded us that God had sent him. There is certainly power in prayer, so many people were praying for me.

"HE SENT HIS WORD AND HEALED ME"

The hospital was adding a new wing, but I was in the old part and in a semi private room which was the only thing available when I got there. I had a miserable night, and in the morning, the doctor ordered a private room which was a brand new room. It was so light and airy. A room that I could have enjoyed under different circumstances, but God was about to make a special delivery in that room! All day I lay there not able to move. If I slid down in the bed, two nurses had to pull me back up. I have always been independent, and now I could do nothing on my own. When night came the nurse came in and talked awhile, and Bobby lay back in his little make out bed, and the lights were out. I just silently prayed, God if I have to be like this the rest of my life, I wish you would just let me go to sleep and not wake up. Well sometime in my sleep, a computer monitor came up before me. This was before I was acquainted with computers. The computer started printing line upon line until the total monitor was filled. I didn't understand the writing, but the green cursor light went back to the beginning and the "Holy Spirit" started interpreting the message to me. Jesus had sent me a word by the Holy Ghost! He was very personal, and knowing my feelings, said "YOU ARE HEALED" He told me that Bobby would have peace .There were two chairs in the room, and the nurses had picked me up during the day to let me sit up, and then pick me back up for the bed. There was no way I could walk to the chairs and sit down. Then the Holy Spirit told me to wake Bobby, take him by the hand, and you both go and sit in the two chairs. I want to show you that you can sit in those chairs and get up. The visit didn't stop there, but I will tell you what happened then. I woke from my sleep, this visitation kept going over in my mind, I was astonished! It was so real! I pondered if I should wait until morning to tell Bobby, but after a short while, the Holy Spirit was in that room so strong. I just felt his presence so much, I called Bobby, and he was quick to answer. By now, I was trembling, and crying and trying to tell him what had happened. The rails were up on each side of the bed, and somehow, I slid over to the edge of the bed and hung my feet over. He said well, let's do what he said do. Believe me when I say the Holy Spirit can speak to you! I let my feet touch the floor, and stood up holding on to Bobby. We walked to the chairs, sat down, and got up. That's when the shouting started! We walked around in the room by the light that was shining from a street light outside. We praised God over and over and over. God had started the "Healing" then. I didn't look healed, my feet were still swollen, and I was still weak but I knew without any doubt, that my healing had begun. And I began to tell everybody that visited me. They might have thought I had been out of my mind. But my mind was very clear, and I knew that I knew, my healing was on the way. I have given my testimony to many people and I have never had anyone tell me they didn't believe it. God gets the Glory!

"MESSAGE FOR THE CHURCH"

He showed me a church full of people. It looked like a sea of people, no faces were visible. Then he said a shocking thing. He said the church doesn't love me. They are PLAYING church with a party spirit. He then said they have left, but when they come back they will be filled with the Holy Spirit. This sounded like the message he gave to the church at Ephesus, in Revelation. He saw their good deeds and works, but he said I have somewhat against you. You have left your first love. Working only because of duty, not love for me. The playing church reminded me of how I use to make play houses when I was a child. We would move to a new house, and I would look the yard over to find a good place for me to make a play house. That was my recreation. I would find bricks and short planks, etc and make my belief furniture. I would make my piano first, because music was important in my life and I liked to think I could play and sing. Which I would do with gusto! A stove to cook on because I wanted to make cakes with mud and pour it into the Luzzianne coffee can lids which were my pans. I made everything just like a real house, but it was a "Play" house. Churches today are set up properly with everything resembling a place of worship, which I like too. But what we really need is the real Holy Spirit filled church like Jesus taught in the gospel of Acts. The visit went on and the talking stopped but then it was spirit to spirit language. I knew what he was saying without hearing it in words. He said the church age was close to the end, and I heard emphasis put on a phrase that I kept hearing over and over. "It's like your sixth finger and your sixth vertebrae" I heard, but I did not understand it, and I still don't. I do know that the giants in the Bible had six toes and six fingers. Then he showed me the head of a pastor, which I will not name which had come to a church. A wolf in sheep's clothing. He told me something "Strange" was going to happen to him. That was a very important visit, one I will never forget. I had a promise sent from God. You are healed! When I share this, I still feel the presence of the Holy Spirit as he talked to me in the hospital.

"BLOOD POISON IN THE BLOOD"

The infectious disease doctor had to check my blood before I left the hospital. Then he told me I had Salmonella blood poisoning. When he explained this to me I knew I had come very close to death. After being released from the hospital, I had to go back to my cancer doctor. This time he gave me my final report. He had given up all hopes of me getting well. He looked at me in the wheelchair and said you're getting weaker and weaker, and your legs and feet are still swollen, you will just get worst. He gave me the choice of taking another chemo treatment if I wanted to, but Bobby and I chose not to. From that time until now, I have not taken any thing for cancer or amyloidosis. When I read Proverbs, I knew it was impossible for me to have cancer and health both in my bone marrow. Remember Jesus had sent me a message, you are healed! Why would I look like I wasn't healed? Well it was a walk of faith the rest of that year.

"GOD GETS THE GLORY"

Now it's up to me. Doctors can't do anything, and God said it's already done. That's when God gets the glory. I was having lots of visitors. And I was sharing my testimony with each of them. The mailbox would be full of get well cards each day, some from people I had never known. I would open them until my strength was gone, then Bobby would open for me. Friends were sending flowers, and bringing food. We appreciated each act of kindness, but the love of the people would make me cry, which I did so much. Bobby was truly an angel to me. He completely stopped doing anything outside the house, he would only leave me long enough to go to the grocery store. A former pastor, Jesse Ogden and wife Patricia, came a long distance to visit and pray for me. They have always been dedicated to the cause of Christ, and special in our lives. We appreciated that so much. A preacher, Curtis Scott and family visited and prayed with us often. We will never forget their kindnesses.

"LOTION KEEPS COMING IN"

Mary, my sister knew of my suffering with the itching from the liver problem. She kept me supplied with the Evelyn Crabapple lotion. In the late evening and night, I was tormented with the nerve itching. Bobby would massage me two or three times each night with the lotion, so I could rest some. If that wasn't enough, I had a case of chicken pox too. Between the two, I would almost go crazy. "That calls for a real walk of faith" he would take me for some evening rides in the car, thinking that might help me some. I still had no strength in my back and feet. But he put a wheel chair ramp at our back door to roll me out to the car. As we would ride around, I would see people running and playing, going up and down steps. I wondered quietly, are they realizing how blessed they are? I was in a wheelchair for a good while. I would go to the hospice doctor, and have lab work, just to please my family doctor. I was getting lab copies each trip and I would compare them to the last ones. Something started showing up. Each one looked closer to normal. Then I graduated to a walker. I would take each step in the name of "Jesus" my liver enzymes were much improved, No jaundice, my appetite was good, and no more heart burn. I started looking for calories, so I could gain some of that lost weight back. I was beginning to walk on my own, with just a little help from Bobby. I had to repent of a saying I had made in the past when I would see older folks holding hands when they were walking. I'd say I bet it's his second wife. But Bobby, my only husband went through the suffering and pain with me. He was a real Angel! Mary continually sent gifts and flowers to me. So many of our families and friends cooked meals and brought them to us. All of the prayers for us were appreciated. Everybody were so good to us, I cried many tears of thanksgiving for them. My three sisters would bring complete meals and visit with us. All of these kindnesses were much appreciated.

"THE WHEELCHAIR RAMP COMES DOWN"

It was recommended by my doctor to sign up with the hospice care. After months of going to the hospice cancer doctor, He remarked Mrs. Brown it's amazing how good you are doing with no medication. That's when I asked for another bone marrow test. So the last month that I went to him, two good things happened to me. I was old enough to "draw" my social security and I had the bone marrow test. When the report came back, this is what it said. "No cancer cells were detected, and bone was of good structure." Just what we expected! We could hardly wait until we got home so Bobby could make some phone calls. My swelling had gone down and I could hold my own glass to drink. I had enough strength in my hands that I could sign my name. Bobby had been made my power of attorney. I was having so many opportunities to give my healing testimony to the people I was meeting. Bobby was calling all the people he could think of that had been interested in my healing. This was the last of November 1996, and that was a wonderful Christmas gift for us. I had come through the worst of my trial period. When the healing started in my body, Satan did not give up easily. But we still believed the promises of God. Remember "Truth" or "Facts" Now Bobby had the privilege to take down the wheelchair ramp.

"THE LORD IS MY SHEPHERD"

The Lord is my shepherd: I shall not want. He maketh me to lie down in green pastures; he leadeth me beside the still water. He restoreth my soul; he leadeth me in the paths of righteousness for his name's sake. Yea, though I walk through the valley of the shadow of death, I will fear no evil; For thou art with me; thy rod and thy staff they comfort me. Thou preparest a table before me in the presence of mine enemies: Thou anointest my head with oil; My cup runneth over. Surely goodness and mercy shall follow me all the days of my life: and I will dwell in the house of the Lord for ever. Psalm 23

"A TIME FOR EYE CHECK-UP"

It had been some time since I had been to see my optometrist, so now I would get another opportunity to give my healing testimony. I explained why I had not been to see him in a long time, and the conversation went on in to my testimony. He got so interested in it he wanted to hear more. So when I went back a week later to pick up some new glasses, he had a tape recorder in his office. He asked me if I would just record the things I had told him, so I gladly accepted. Then he told me about a meeting with my cancer doctor a few nights before and said he wants you to come by and let him see you. This was another good opportunity. This time I had the privilege of telling him my whole story. I told him of my spiritual visitation in the hospital, and the scripture verses I was reminded of and trusted in. He just looked and listened to me. He said one thing I remember about you was you never got upset when I gave you the report. Action speaks louder than words! My family doctor told me in all her years of practice, she had never seen a case like mine, and now she too calls me a miracle.

"RESTORATION"

God has restored all the things the canker worm and the palmer worm has eaten away. Or in other words what the devil tried to steal from us. And we thank him for that. Even though we had no income during this period in our lives, we were able to pay every medical bill. Now it was time to build a new building where the old one burned, and business would go on. Bobby and I would take our usual places there. Now in 2007, we are still going to work each day! My office is my pulpit and I give my testimony to any one when the Holy Spirit prompts me. To God Be the Glory! You may ask the question why did you get healed and others did not. But I would ask you a question too. When Samuel went to Jesse' house to anoint a King, Jesse's 7 sons that seemed to be excellent candidates for the kingship marched before him but Samuel asked, are there any more sons in the family? He said only one more and he's tending the sheep. But when he was sent for, the little shepherd boy was anointed King David. I don't have answers but Acts 10:3 tells me that God is no respecter of persons. He looks on the heart and not on the outward appearance.

IN LOVING MEMORIES OF OUR PARENTS

Corine and Walter Moon

and

Carrie and James Brown

Who loved us and cared for us the best they could in difficult situations during the depression years when the resources were few.

PART 2:

"MEMORIES OF MY CHILDHOOD"

(And family lives in short stories)

"BEGINS IN 1933"

Back in January of 1933, a little girl was born in Madison, Georgia in the rural area of Morgan County. I suppose it was an insignificant occasion, since I was born during the great depression years. Times were very hard on poor people. Years went by before I would realize that. But in time, I just knew we were poor and was very careful not to waste anything that we had. I didn't know that the cotton mattresses that we slept on were hand made by my parents until later. And the can food for winter that we ate was raised by our family and was canned by them locally at a place in Madison. But I remember going with daddy one day to the cannery. I knew we had only kerosene lamps to light our house, and they were used sparingly. At early dark they were blown out to save the kerosene. We later got an Aladdin lamp but it too used kerosene. We didn't have any electricity so we had to draw our water from a well and if we needed to keep anything cool, it was lowered into the well in the bucket for a while. Fresh water from the well was our beverage at meal time. When clothes were washed, a big black pot was filled with well water and heated by a fire that was built around it. A rub board was put in a tub of water and clothes were scrubbed with mama's hands. When week-end baths were needed, a wash tub of water was put in the sun outside long enough to be heated some and brought in the house. We had a privy outside with the old "Sears Roebuck" catalog hanging in the corner. When clothes were ironed, a real iron was heated on the wood stove or fireplace, and it was pure luck if a garment was finished without a suet spot on it. We had a radio that was operated by a battery, and it was not turned on unless some news or the "Grand Ole

Opry" was on Saturday nights. We all would gather around and look straight at the radio. When the programs went off the radio was off too. Gasoline was rationed, but the five gallons of gas would take us all the places we needed to go. Our house was heated in the winter time with a fireplace and kitchen stove. Our bedrooms were quite cold but we had plenty of quilts. In the summer time, people were usually supplied with hand fans donated by funeral homes, but that didn't stop much sweating. No matter how hot it was, the meals were prepared on a wood burning stove. Windows and outside doors were always open, hoping for a good breeze to blow by.

I only thought that was the way of life. But in the year of '33, The WPA recovery act was passed by Pres. Roosevelt. Also the CCC camp at near by Rutledge, Georgia was a place the men could work with income to survive. I was born in this time, and only knew of the times when families were trying to get over the deep depression. These created jobs were a blessing to many. The rich landowners lived much above their farm families, and were highly respected. I was born on the Carmichael Farm. So that was the first house of my remembrance. The sister that was 6 years older than I was Marjorie, and we played some together, but I don't remember much of those years. I do remember a junk car parked between our house and the barns, and I loved to play in it. I was about four years old, and liked to move all the parts on the dash of the car and pretend I was driving, blowing the horn, and pulling the throttle out. But one day I was attacked by a wasp and I ran home to mama for relief. She had a dip of snuff in her mouth, so she took some of that and put on the stinging place for the pain. That was always a remedy for any place that hurt. I don't ever remember seeing any pain medication in the house. Before my mother was married, she had gone to the A & M College in Madison for a time, she was better educated than my daddy, but she believed in letting the man take his rightful place as the head of the house. My birthday came early in the year, so I was enrolled in school at Madison when I was five years old. My daddy never had a degree in hair dressing, but he knew how to use scissors to cut hair. At least that's what he thought. Since I was about to go to school, he wanted to have my hair neatly trimmed. He would cut my bangs, then the sides to the bottom of my ear lobes. Then he would step back and say to me, now I'm going to trim it up. Which meant it was uneven and it was going to be even shorter. I didn't like it but that didn't matter to him. I would be clean looking. I had dimples when I smiled, which I hated, and my ears always stuck out from underneath my cotton white hair. But every picture that was made of me in the first grade I was always smiling big, so it didn't bother my ego.

"FIRST SCHOOL DAYS"

When the big yellow bus came by our house, I was always ready to hop in. My first grade teacher was Miss Hart, and I thought she was so pretty. I remember the dress she wore the first day. It was black with white trim. I was quite and bashful. But I was a good student, and not inclined to bother any body. We sat in our own seats that were assigned to us. And I was put right behind a boy. One day he kept turning around and messing with my neat desk top. I kept my tablet and pencil and stuff right in place, and I kept telling him to quit, but he did not heed the warnings, so I hit him. Then his commotion caused the teacher to look, and I was the one that got the punishment. The boy didn't get any. The punishment for that crime was to stand in the corner. I was so embarrassed I couldn't look at the others. I had a hair clasp in my hair and I would put it in, and take it out, over and over. I would have stuck my tongue out at him, which I usually did if I didn't like what somebody did. But I knew that would get me in more trouble. That was my last punishment at school. Some of the mothers were called "grade mothers." They would come and help with special occasions. I well remember Mrs. Vason. She always brought pretty trays of decorated goodies. She too was a very pretty lady. The building now is known as the Cultural Center. The whole yard was dirt. If the girls got to school a little early, we would run to the "skin the cat pole." I loved to play on that. There were swings, see-saws and a long fire escape we could go up and slide down. We played hop scotch and jump rope. The boys would make circles, and play marbles, or spin their tops. There was lots of play space. But when that bell rung, we would run and line up to walk inside. Discipline was abided by and misbehaving was not tolerated. Our teachers were well respected. We knew not to go inside with chewing gum in our mouths. That was a "no-no." I started to school at the age of five and graduated at the age of sixteen all at the same school.

"A BIG SURPRISE"

After a few months at school, my mama sent my older sister and me to our neighbor's house for a visit. I didn't think anything strange about that because I liked to go to Mr. and Mrs. Pace's house. Mr. Pace always took time to play with me. When time to go back home, we headed up the dirt road, which now is the busy Hwy. 441, not knowing there was a big surprise at our house. When we walked in, mama was in bed, and that was strange, because mama never went to bed in the day time. On top of that, a dresser drawer was at the bottom of the bed with a blanket in it. Low and behold, a baby was in it. My baby sister, Mary had been born. I had no idea we would be having a baby at our house. Carrie Jackson, a black lady that our family loved a lots was there to do our cooking and looking after mama for a while. She carried Mary around the house saying the first one that carries the baby around the house, the baby will take after them. By then I was 6 years old but I had not noticed that mama looked different. I just thought that was the way she was supposed to look. Now I was not the baby any more, I was going to school and getting educated, so I had to help look after Mary somewhat. At that time we were thought of as living in the country with a dirt road, but now there is a Kentucky Chicken restaurant there in that location, plus many more businesses. While we lived there, we went to the Presbyterian Church in Madison. I always believed in God, and enjoyed Sunday school and Bible school in the summer. A lady from the church would pick us up and take us to the church Bible school. At Christmas time, they would have a Christmas tree, and give out gift bags of fruit and candy to the children. I still remember how we would play on the little street wall in front of the church after the service was over, and the grown ups would talk. The wall is still standing today.

"AT THE CARMICHAEL FARM"

Daddy worked in a shop at the barns keeping the farm tools repaired and doing the other necessary things. It was inside a fenced in pasture. I didn't like to go inside the fence because there was a bad hog wondering around in there. I would look all around for the animals before I would crawl under the wire fence to go in to see daddy. But one day I got caught between the fence and the barn by the bad hog. I hollered for daddy and barely made it back to the fence before it got me. Daddy rescued me. My older sister and I did something our family didn't know about. During peach season, there would be big loads of peaches brought to the farm and unloaded over the fence for the hogs. We would watch for the trucks, and if the hogs were not around, we would go over the fence and get some of the nice big peaches. They just looked too good to let the hogs have all of them. We would eat until we were full. I know we would have been spanked if they had known. Daddy looked after some cotton fields there too. There was cotton to be picked, and I wanted to pick some too, so mama made me a small cotton picking sack. I would go to the field with the rest of them with my little sack, but one night I forgot and left it on the back porch and the pet goat chewed it up. Mama would get so aggravated with that goat, and finally said it's got to go.

"THE HAUNTED HOUSE"

We moved to another house. This one was known to be the haunted house. Our family didn't believe it because our family was never superstitious. But mama, daddy and Christine, the oldest sister all had things happen that could not be explained. The front door had a different sound from the other doors when it opened. Mama would be in the kitchen and hear the door open, and just thinking the wind had blown it open, she would go to shut it. But the door would be already closed. This occasion happened frequently. The night before we were to move, mama and daddy had the dishes and breakable things wrapped and in barrels. Daddy heard the barrels roll up and down the big wide hall all night, he just knew everything would be broken the next morning, but when he looked nothing had been moved. Then he wondered about the "HAUNTS." We were stilled going to the Presbyterian Church and most of the time mama would stay home and have a delicious dinner cooked for us when church was over. Sunday dinners were always special. This was the time of sugar and gas rationing, and we only could have sweet tea on Sunday. On Saturday, we would always go by the Ice House in Madison and get a fifty pound block of ice and carry it home on the running board of our car. That would keep over the week-end wrapped up on the back porch. The Ice House is different now there's no ice anymore, but condos, restaurants, and gift shops. Now when we go to Madison, it brings back many memories. Daddy always had a good garden and mama was a real good cook and meal planner. At church there were two boys that always begged to go home with us and have Sunday dinner. Most of the time their parents would gladly let them go with us. They said we can't have but one glass of sweet tea at home, but mama said we could have all we wanted when we went off. They were rough with our toys and we would try to hide them, but they would look until they found them. We didn't have a bath room in the house but daddy would always build us a new outside privy with three seats in it when we moved to a new place. One was for the adults, one for the middle size and one for the little folks. The oldest boy never failed to eat a while then say excuse me, I'll be right back. He would take off to the privy quickly and right back again for more. Aunt Jane, a black woman lived by her self in a little shack above our house. She was almost blind and stayed in bed, and after we would eat, my sister and I would always take her lunch and a quart of sweet tea. We would call her, and after a long wait she would come to the door. She was always so happy to get a nice meal.

"FRIEDMAN'S DRY GOOD STORE"

When we needed clothes if mama couldn't repair what we had, we were always taken to Madison to "Friedmans" store. We didn't tell our parents what to buy. They bought the things that was available and what they could pay for. No credit cards back then. I remember one year getting school shoes. I ended up with a pair of wedge heels which was red, white and blue. The kind you would wear now on the 4th of July. I hated them but I wore them without a fuss. Mama was pretty good at her petal sewing machine and she made most of our clothes, but since I was the middle child, I wore mostly hand me downs. Sometimes they fit, and sometimes I just wore them anyway. We were always excited when we collected several flour sacks that were alike. Somebody would get a new dress. The flour sacks were quite attractive sometimes. We looked forward to using the last of the flour so the sacks could be washed and used for clothes. Friedman's store was later sold and the last one was Mack's Dept store, and now there are no dry good stores in Madison.

"LARGE COTTON FARMS"

At this farm cotton was the main crop. My job was to keep water to the choppers and later to the pickers. At certain times of day, I would fill a bucket with fresh water and go to each person. They would be so glad to see me coming. We lived in the big house, and had a little store on the back of the house. It was filled with things some of the workers would need. One of the items was snuff. One day I was taking snuff to one person. It was a square container I don't remember the name and it smelled so good, I decided to taste it so I took off the lid and licked my finger and touched it, but the smell was disguising. It tasted awful. Snuff and tobacco was common among country folk. Daddy plowed some in new fields of corn, and when I would take him water sometimes he would tell me to bring a jar of vanilla milk on the next trip. Mama could fix some of the best vanilla milk you ever tasted. It was sweet and she would put a little ice in it. At that time we had gotten a nice ice box refrigerator and had ice more often. I would start off taking the milk to daddy, and I would stop and take a few sips. I would go a little farther, and the temptation was so great, I would take another sip. I would shake it up hoping it didn't show that I had been drinking some. Mr. Ernest Ward was our ice delivery man. He would bring us a 50 lbs block of ice at a time. He would bring it in with hooks, and one day the hooks slipped off and it fell on his foot. We felt bad about it, but I always think of that when I see Mr. Ward. Of course, after it was over with, we couldn't keep from laughing. When the cotton pickers stopped picking at the end of day, it would be weighted and marked on a book until pay day. Daddy had a mule that liked to run away if any thing scared it. One day he was hooked to a sled that had brought baskets of cotton to the storage house, and all of a sudden he started running away, bouncing the sled until it got loose. He ran down the road and daddy started after him. Since he had no boys, I was expected to do boy things, so he told me to stand at the road leading into the yard and head the mule off. I didn't like the idea, but I thought I'd better do what he told me to. I got a broom and got in the road, waving it up in the air, hoping it would turn before he got to me. The mule started up the road toward me with his ears laid back and running wide open, and my legs would not let me stay still. I threw the broom down and headed for the house as fast as I could go. There was no way I would try to stop this animal.

"CHORES ALWAYS"

At the big house, we had a hand pump on the well and a wash house separate from the big house. I was old enough now to help with cleaning the diapers. There were no pampers then, only cloth diapers and that was a job I hated. But a tub would be filled with water and a load of dirty diapers for me to wash for Mary. Some would cause me to gag. After washing and rinsing the diapers, they would be hung on the clothes line to dry. We had a cook stove that was fired up with wood, and daddy seemed to like to cut stove wood. And he believed in having an excessive amount of wood cut. After we carried enough inside the house, we would have to stack more up on the porch. We were always busy doing some chores around the house. The corn crib would be full of corn to be shucked and shelled. And if nothing else was urgent, we would be sent to the crib. Daddy operated a corn grinding mill at Carmichael's lake, and we had some of the best corn bread. I would walk down to the mill and was amazed watching the big water wheel turn and throw off the water, and smell the good smell of corn grinding. One day as I was walking home from the mill, I saw some big white flowers growing by the side of the road, so I picked a bouquet for mama. In a short time, daddy drove by and picked me up in his truck. Soon afterwards bees started coming out of the blooms, and I had to throw my flowers out of the window to get rid of them. Mama had no cut flowers that day.

"FUN GROWING UP"

I had so much fun growing up on the farm. I liked to wear over-hauls with lots of pockets. I would fill each one with something. I didn't have lots of playmates since the sister next to me was six years older. But I could just have fun all by myself. I would always find a favorite spot in the yard to make a "play house." I would gather little scraps of lumber, old bricks and go to work building my make belief furniture. I always had a cook stove and would place it in a sunny spot so it would get hot. I made mud cakes and used "Luzziane" coffee can lids for pans. There were always berries growing close by and they would be my peas and a piano was always made. Everything was there to resemble a real house. I would sit at my piano and sing to my heart's desire. I would make tom walkers to make me much taller, and cut holes in large tin cans, and tie them to my shoes. That too would make me taller. But as I got older, I grew taller than I wanted to. On warm days mama would sit on the front porch after dinner. Maybe a neighbor would come by and they would talk and spit their snuff. I would start begging mama to let me go swimming in the lake. Finally one day she allowed me to go with my two older sisters. I was feeling pretty secure and inched on out in the water and suddenly I couldn't feel the bottom. I was really getting into trouble, but my sister got to me just in time. It liked to have scared me to death and I never learned to swim. I liked the water but I would prefer fishing over swim-ming. I could go fishing alone and not be afraid. I wouldn't have a pole or hook, but I would find a pretty straight limb and add a string with a crooked pin. I could always find plenty of worms for bait, and I would be ready to go fishing in the little creek below us. I could hook one in the side pretty good. I never had any fish to take home, but I enjoyed sitting on the bank and getting the nibbles. I could have been called a tom-boy.

"SPIT IN THE FACE"

The back of our house was high off the ground, and the porch was boxed up about three feet. It was hard to see over it. There was an opening at the end where the steps came up. Mama always went to that corner to spit her snuff. Our driveway ran right beside the back porch, and the people that lived on the farm would walk by coming and going. One day this black woman was coming by and mama didn't know anybody was around, but just as she spit, the woman heard someone walking on the porch and looked up, but it was too late, Mama had just let it go. It hit her right in the face. Mama apologized but really couldn't keep from laughing after it was over with. We had some good black people that lived around us, and I always enjoyed visiting with them. One was Sarah Lankford. She did lots of quilting, but she had bad eye site and I would go to her house and sit at the table and thread her needle for her. She had a big black pot in the back yard and cooked her soap in it. The room I liked most was wall papered with magazine pictures. She always kept her house clean. I enjoyed my visits with Sarah. The house we lived in was built for someone from New York we were told. We were also told that someone was killed in it. Maybe that was the reason for the "Haunts." Each door was adorned with beautiful art paintings, and the ceiling light fixtures were too. People were always coming by to see the paintings. I always admired art and liked the paintings. But mama would get a little annoyed when so many people would come by to see them. She always worried something might be out of place when people came by, and she always wanted to have the house presentable.

"BARTERING"

We could take milk and eggs to school, and swap them for tickets to the lunch room. We were taught responsibility early, and we didn't loose our tickets. Daddy had things in the garden that a grocery store owner would come out and buy. I remember him getting truck loads of cabbages, extra large for 4 cents each. People on the farm helped each other too. You could take your corn to the mill and have it ground and pay for it with some of the meal. Bartering was a good thing when there was no money. Times were hard during the depression years but we always had plenty to eat because daddy always raised it in a garden and our family was small. We ate mostly pork, because he always had a good hog and in the cold winters they would have a hog killing time, and lay the meat up on a tin roof over night in the cold weather so it wouldn't ruin and wild animals couldn't get to it. All the neighbors got some of the meat at each killing, and a salt box was made to hold the side meat covered over with salt. If cholesterol existed then, no one knew it. We always had one cow that gave us the milk and butter and plenty hens in the hen house for our eggs. As soon as a hen would lay a egg, she would let out a cackle, then we knew to run and get it. The chickens had to be guarded from the wild animals. When margarine showed up in the grocery stores it was white and had to be mixed with a little packet of orange coloring. We thought that was the worst tasting stuff ever. I was too little to know just how bad the depression was. I just knew we all lived like the neighbors. If anything had to be bought with money, it was used sparingly. We learned to be thrifty. Our cook stove had a warming closet on it, and when we would come from school there would always be something in it for us to eat. The rest was left for supper. Sometimes it would be a sweet potato or if mama had a craving for something sweet, she would have a big plate of tea cakes with chocolate icing setting on the table. That was my favorite.

"OUR THIRD MOVE"

Daddy changed jobs. This time he went from a cotton farm to a dairy farm. This time my job was washing up the barn, carrying milk to the milk house, and putting feed in the troughs for the cows. It was the "Wilson" farm. Again I helped after school each day. We lived above the Wilson House, and they had a bad dog named "Hitler." I would have to walk through their yard to get to the barn. And before I would get to their house, my heart would be racing, I was so afraid "Hitler" would get me. He never bit me, but I never trusted him either. They had a son named John, and we had lots of fun playing together. We would ride their bull calves and horse. He had a horse that he would hitch to the buggy and we would ride all over the place. We were always gathering old materials together to build huts next to the creek. One day as we were gathering old planks and rusty nails that we could straighten out, I stepped on a nail. It soon got bad when a red streak started up my leg, and I had to go to a doctor. I overheard my parents say it looks like blood poisoning, and I knew that was dangerous. John had a pretty bad temper, and if his horse didn't do just what he wanted it do, he could use some pretty bad language, I never did like that. He liked the western picture shows, especially "Roy Rogers." One day we got the idea that we could make a Ferris wheel. John's grandpa, that he called Popeye, would give him anything that he asked for. So he let us have some nice wood and metal pipes. We worked for days on it and finally the try out day came. It had a seat at the top and one at the bottom. The person on the bottom would push off, and it would make several loops before stopping. We really had some good times on the

"Ferris Wheel." At this time, Mary was old enough to go to school. Mama made her a yellow pinafore to wear. And platting her hair was done each morning. It was like warfare to Mary just seeing the comb and brush lying beside the rubber bands that would go on the ends. Little did we know how she would hate to go to school, But she would start soon as mama got her hair platted saying it's too tight. Then she would cry not wanting to go to school. But she would always get on the bus. By recess time I would always get the message, your little sister is crying and there would be a big crowd around her wanting to see. I hated to go in the crowd and talk to her. Her teacher Mrs. Fleming called her the little yellow butterfly. But that didn't help Mary. She probably wished she had been a butterfly so she could fly away and never return to school.

"MY FIRST BIG JOB"

We lived close to Hwy 441, and I had gotten a job at "Armour's" Five and Ten cents store. I was only twelve years old. The "Greyhound" bus was the only way I could get to my job. So I would go down to the highway and wave the bus down. The nice driver always recognized me and would stop and let me sit on the cover of the engine for five cents and ride in to Madison. This was a Saturday job. At lunch time, the Madison Drug Store was just down the street, and I would always have my lunch there. It was always a pimento cheese sandwich with chips and a coca cola. I felt pretty big working in Madison and eating at a drug store. Now every time I eat a toasted cheese sandwich, I remember the old days. Madison was the place where everybody went on Saturday. It usually was a day of seeing their neighbors and friends and buying their week's supply of everything. Daddy had bought a little Ford car with a rumble seat. I was getting to the age when I was embarrassed to be seen in the rumble seat but daddy was real proud of his car, and $1.50 worth of gas would last a long time with some riding on Sunday evenings to see kin folks. At Christmas, the Armour's would always present me with a gift which usually was a puzzle. Stores would always close at nine o'clock on Saturdays. One of my duties was to always sweep off the walk in front of the store, by that time everybody would be clearing out and headed home.

"CHRISTMAS TIMES"

Mama would always get as excited about Christmas as we did. She would start collecting candies and making cakes weeks before Christmas. She loved chocolate covered cherries, and that was always on her list of candy. She would keep a large box stored underneath the bed, and we knew not to touch it. That's where she kept her Christmas goodies. She would order the famous "Sears Roebuck" fruit cake. And would make at least five cakes and store them away until Christmas morning. That's when she would cut each one, and that would be our breakfast that morning. One year she ordered a bucket of hard candy, and she got that one plus a second bucket came by accident to us. We had candy long after Christmas that year. She would clean house and we would go Christmas tree hunting. It was hard to find a perfect tree, but if it was a little one sided we would just turn that side to the wall. It was a must to get some holly with berries. The house was decorated with all the decorations we kept from year to year. We had little red crepe paper bells that folded and un-folded to hang in the windows and the icicles and roping for the tree was always saved. On Christmas Eve night, each of us would hang one of mama's old cotton stockings on the fireplace. When morning came, daddy would make a roaring fire before we got up and our eyes would just light up as we saw those stockings almost touching the fireplace with a apple, orange, raisins on the stalk, a big peppermint stick, sparklers and small fire crackers. Daddy would get a shovel of hot coals and take them to the porch, and there we would shoot off our fireworks. His way of celebrating was to shoot his gun in the air several times. We didn't get many toys, it was mostly school clothes. Mama ordered many things from the "Spiegel" catalog. I remember the "Sonja Henny" hat that was so popular and I got one. I always had "Jophers" on my list too. That was my favorite attire. I was so comfortable in them with the leather patches inside the knees which were big at the hips and tight from knees down to my feet.

"DADDY BUYS HIS OWN LITTLE HOUSE"

This little house with four acres of land was for sell. This was a house that mama and daddy had lived in their early marriage. Daddy had wanted it so bad. The cedar tree that mama remembered walking by on the way to school when she was young was still standing in the yard. Well the day came that he bought it. The weeds were up waist high in the yard, and the inside had to be worked on lots. But he started collected odds and ends to finish the inside, and he and mama were so happy. You would have thought he had acquired a mansion. He would work on his own now. He liked to paint, so he started painting houses for others. We had no well, but he thought he would just dig his own well, and so he did. Their only son had died at a few months old with diphtheria, so I was treated somewhat like a boy. I would slip out there and go down the ladder into the well sometimes and dig a little. I remember how cool it was down there. He didn't have to go real deep before he had water. But before the well was dug, He had a mule and a sled to haul water on from a neighbor's house. I liked to hitch up the mule and drive it down the road with the big cans to get water. That was a pretty big job to draw enough water to fill those cans but I liked to drive that mule. He was very gentle, always walking at the same pace.

I would help mama put up some sheetrock and wallpaper in the house when time permitted. We would struggle with heavy sheetrock and get tickled about how we were doing it. We could just see in our mind's eye that we would have a pretty wall some day. In the beginning of Spring I would go with mama to the white mud hole. The women always found one close by. We would take a bucket and get it full. Mama would clean all the ashes out of the fireplace and the white mud was just like paint. She would paint the fireplace and hearth with it. That would really brighten the room up. She always stayed home and kept the house in order and cooked the meals. Daddy always expected to have supper ready when he came in from work and mama always had it ready for the table. Daddy had a very good garden spot, and he loved to work in it too. After his paint work in the spring and summer months, he would eat his supper and go straight to the garden, and it paid off well with vegetables.

"MY SEVENTH GRADE AT SCHOOL"

My teacher was Mrs. Bell. This was the last class before high school. She was pretty easily upset and when she did get upset, she would turn a purplish color. Some of the boys would do things that would call for punishment. They liked to see her turn purple, but she would make the trouble maker go and break a switch from the bushes that grew outside and then she switched him in front of the class. The idea for going to school was to be taught, and all of my teachers adhered to the same rules. When we got good grades, we had truly earned them. We were now getting ready for the eighth grade and it was pretty tough. The summer was spent anticipating the next year, where we would have special classes and many more books to carry in our arms. We had no idea that the high school building would burn down soon and we would be moved to the old "A & M" college buildings. But it happened any way. We used the old buildings that my mama had probably been taught in while she was in A & M School. But there I would graduate in 1949, and would enter a new kind of life.

"SCHOOL PALS"

The last of our high school years, I remember some of my closest friends and I would sit by a window at the last period waiting for the bell to ring, and we would have some tall plans for our lives after school. Of course my plans were to marry Bobby. We would see George ride through the school grounds waiting to see Dorothy, but we didn't know they would be married soon too. Bennie Mae didn't tell us her plans, but I imagine she had her eyes on W.R. then. Daisy Lee was a character and half, she knew my name was Gertrude Clopton Moon and she knew how much I hated it, and she had to ask Bobby if he knew what my whole name was. She kept us laughing all the time. Beatrice couldn't talk about anybody but Erland, we didn't know him, but she knew she was going to get him. Mattinee didn't tell us her plans, but later on somebody saw her looking at a boy riding a motorcycle and she fell for Bill. Mary Anne already had her school mate Lamar picked out, and they married shortly. Many years have gone since then, but the good memories still linger on of our school friends.

"A GRADUATION GIFT"

One evening after school, I was leaving the post office in Madison with a load of books in my arms when I met the "Prince Charming" of my life. He was a very cute, curly headed boy. I was going to a Ten Cents Store that my sister Marjorie was managing. He happened by and offered to take my books and drive me home. That began a new chapter in my life. After several months of dating, He asked me to marry him. I learned later that he had prayed for a wife. So for my graduation gift from him I received the engagement ring. Two months later, we were taken to a minister's house on a Sunday morning and were married. Mama had made me a two piece white dress for the wedding, and Bobby wore dress pants, white shirt and tie. I had never been to a wedding before and when the minister said join right hands, I was on Bobby's right side, and I thought "something" is wrong, guess I must be on the wrong side. But our marriage has lasted 58 years so it must have been done right. Our wedding only cost what Bobby paid the minister.

"OFF TO THE BROWN'S HOUSE"

After our ceremony, we didn't go on a cruise but rather we joined with the whole "Brown Clan" for lunch at their house. All of the Browns were gathered cooking a big meal. People from all around were there. There was so much talking and I was not use to so much commotion. They enjoyed talking more than eating. I pondered in my heart, had I made the right choice getting into this? But they all welcomed me into the family. After some time, the table was spread with everything you could think of. They fixed everything at least three different kind of ways. After a long stay with them we went to our apartment already furnished with basic furniture from "Harris Furniture Store" which was bought on terms. This was the year of nineteen hundred, forty nine and the effects from the depression were still being felt. We lived in down town Madison, with a walking distance to the stores, and to the movie theater. Bobby had a job at the "International Furniture Co." making less than a dollar an hour. Later I got a job at "Mendel's Appliance Store." I was making eighteen dollars a week. We both were very young and happy. We didn't own a car, and Bobby started wanting to buy one. His daddy had a car that needed repair, so he bought it and now we had some transportation, as long as we could afford to buy gas for our old Plymouth, we could ride. It needed a paint job bad, so we knew a way to remedy that. Bobby went to the Western Auto and bought a gallon of black paint and some paint brushes from Mr. Truman Prior, and one evening we gave that old car a face lift. It was transformed from a grayish blue to a bright lustrous black. We stood back with amazement and were very proud of our accomplishment. Our lives would be filled with happiness and seasons of sadness. But at this time, we knew nothing but happiness. We didn't care that we had nothing but each other. I washed most of our clothes in the bath tub, and hung them on the close line to dry. Since Bobby was working at the furniture co. we saved enough money to buy a living room suit. That along with some inexpensive end tables furnished our third room.

"LONGING FOR THE COUNTRY LIFE"

Since we both were raised in the country, we were yearning to return. We wanted some open spaces and garden spots, plenty of dirt, grass and trees. We found a house that we liked. It was too big, but we could just close some of it off and use three rooms in it. We rented it right away. It was an old home place with lots of barns and buildings, just what we liked in the Brownwood community. We moved in and just like children, we explored each building and walked over every inch of ground. There was a rich fertile garden spot. We loved that. We must have a garden, but we didn't have a tractor or a mule. Bobby could always work things out, so he acquired a push type plow. This kind had a big wheel in front. That's what we made the prettiest garden in the whole community with. All the people around envied it. Bobby never had a lazy bone in him. We enjoyed walking on the fresh plowed soil, and being in the quietness of the country. In the big white clapboard house I began to have a strange sickness. When I went to the doctor, we found out that I was with child. We were thrilled about the news. And we looked forward to having a little one. But we were about to experience the coldest winter we had ever seen. One night it was so cold, it seemed like a cold breeze was blowing through the house all night, and I kept my head covered with the quilts most of it. Bobby knew how to make a roaring fire, and he kept one burning all night in the fireplace. The next morning I went in to cook breakfast, and my wet cloth froze to the dinette table. Then he cranked the truck to go to work and it was frozen to the ground and would not move. My sickness continued and we decided we were too far from Madison for me to be left alone all day. Bobby began to look for a rental house in Madison. He found a three room house surrounded by a pecan orchard. This suited us so we moved in and the pregnancy went well for eight months. One night I started having flu like symptoms and Bobby called our doctor. He wanted me to see him in the morning, but by morning I needed to go to the hospital. I had RH negative blood and there had been a reaction and the baby that we named Mary Jean was born dead. While I was still in the old "McGeary" hospital, Bobby had to bury our little girl. When I was dismissed from the hospital he took me by "Union Chapel Church" cemetery in Putnam County to see the grave site. By then, all the flowers were wilted, and the sadness was heavy. But this did not make us loose faith in God, We were comforted by him. My sister Marjorie from Griffin, Georgia came and stayed a few weeks with us. She cooked for us and kept the house clean. She was always around when someone needed her. Daddy had some nice vegetables in his garden and every time they would come to see us he would bring something. I remember the nice cabbages he would bring and Marjorie was such a good cook she could make them delicious.

"REVIVAL MEETING"

We heard of a tent revival that was being held in Greensboro. So we decided to attend the meeting. I got out my white two piece dress that mama had made for me to be married in and we went, not knowing that it would be so different from what I was use to. But that night when the preacher got through with his sermon he then gave the altar call and we took each other's hands and went to the front where a bench for set up for the altar. The ground was covered with shavings and we knelt down at the bench and surrendered our lives to God. We had not been bad people, but we knew there was something missing in our lives, which was a real relationship with Jesus. From that time on, we looked at things differently. We had a desire to study the Bible and learn more and more. Bobby started taking a small bible to work with him and he would read during his breaks. Some of the people there didn't understand that, and teased him about it, but it didn't bother him. Finally he got the respect from his fellow workers. Shortly after that, a preacher started coming to see us and would have a tent meeting every year. He was a real scripture teacher from Commerce, Georgia. We always made room for him in our home, even though we didn't have an extra bedroom, we put up a little army cot in our living room for him. We would sit up at night until late just asking questions. We were like two little birds being fed. God was preparing us for the things ahead and he always had scriptural answers. Some of the Pentecostal churches that we went to did things in ignorance that we knew wasn't scriptural. Most of them were fine people, and loved God, but just got carried away in some things that seemed right to them. We enjoyed going to the revival meetings. We would stay late and fellowship with other couples, and on the way home, there was a store called the point that we always stopped by and got the late night treat, the "Ice cream Hunkie." Bobby had bought a new set of tires for our car. We thought they were fine, but evidence proved they had some flaws in that set. We would go off and come back home, and after we would get in the house we would hear a loud noise. It would be another blow out tire. That happened to the whole set.

We both loved music so we borrowed a portable pump organ. I would play hymns in my spare time. I didn't know the sound was being carried blocks away. But I later heard that people were wondering where the music was coming from. Bobby had a guitar and together we could play some pretty good tunes. Later on the boys were in school and I had the opportunity to take piano lessons and learned the basics. I started off with "teaching the little fingers to play" even though I was at a mature age.

"OUR FIRST BUSINESS"

Bobby's salary increased a little and we were feeling very blessed, but we knew we needed to make more money. We kept reaching for another rung of the ladder. Sometimes we would get knocked off again and sometimes holding on. But I have heard it said that a winner is a loser that will not loose. I was very conservative in my buying and we would go to the grocery store and only get the bare necessities. Bobby made the comment that when we got plenty of money we would flatten the tires out on one of those grocery carts. I cooked some very good biscuits and we bought lots of canned corn, some with the pimento peppers in it. Every now and then we would get a pound of bacon which really made it good. If we felt very rich, we would buy a can of roast beef. I didn't believe in wasting so I only cooked the right amount. Our groceries were never over eight dollars a week. The opportunity came for Bobby to buy a small upholstery shop in Madison. He could only get enough money together to buy it, and being in-experienced as we were, we didn't count the cost of operating expenses. We thought this would be the answer for making more money and we sure needed that. He had a painter make a sign for our little business. It looked nice and we were proud to hang it out over the street in front of our business. But the city of Madison had a different opinion. They sent a policeman down and told us it was hanging over the street and could fall on someone. And it must be taken down. The street had other signs hanging too, but we obeyed and took it down. Bobby stood it up on the stairway that led up stairs to his shop. But it was not easily seen and we only made enough money to survive. Bobby started looking for another place to rent, and found one that was suitable. It was right across from the street where I had gone to school. We liked the area and the building too. It was large enough to have a work space plus living quarters too. By this time Bobby had quit his job at the furniture company since he had ventured out in his own business and was working full time in it. He always gave his customers more than he charged for. After much thought to supplement his wages he got a job at the Enterprise Aluminum Co. He could still work nights and week-ends at home, but he never liked that job. When he saw the abuse people were working in, he knew he didn't want that. People had fingers cut off and working with harnesses to keep the work flowing at the expected time which they called a safety feature. The drag ware man was his brother in law, and he dragged the materials to the workers on a sled which seemed to be inhuman. At that time shell casings were being made for the war. He worked just long enough to get his job back at the furniture company. At this time he developed bursitis in his knee, and worked lots in pain and used crutches some. One of his aunts knew about Bobby's Christian walk, and she called him to come to her house and pray for her for some kind of sickness. He thought it over for a while wondering if he should go or not since he was sick too. But he did go and while he was praying for her, the Lord healed the bursitis in his knee too, and he never had any more pain and no more doctor visits with his knee. At this time, we realized we were not ready for the big bad world of high finances with the money we were making. He got his job back at the furniture company this time staying until he was promoted to a Line Foreman. Now his salary increased to a dollar an hour. I got a job at Lunceford's grocery store, and we had two small salaries coming in each week. But the depression was still having some effects on working people.

"TIME OF THE DRAFT AND OUR HOUSE"

The mailman brought some terrible news one day. It was the time of drafting men for the war. This notified Bobby of the time for him to be examined. We were upset to no end. We had been so close during our marriage, and to be torn apart was beyond imagination. But Bobby being the provider, thought of me being all by my self. He would not have that. So he started looking for a place for me. Daddy told us we could build a house close by them. That sounded like an impossible thing but Bobby's mind was made up, he would not leave me without the protection of my folks. We started collecting odds and ends to start building. We were in desperation. We prayed so much about the situation I guess we wearied God for an answer. Bobby went for the examination and we waited for the report. When the answer came he was turned down. We were so imma-ture, we didn't even ask why. We accepted it as an answer to our prayers. But now the house was on the way, so we contin-ued on. Bobby's daddy said he would work on it some. He had helped build the school at Rabin Gap and remembered them putting a Bible in the corner of the building. So he was pretty qualified to do a good job. We told him we would pay him as he worked. Bobby started looking for lumber which was very expensive according to our money, but he found a good deal on some poplar lumber. It was green and when it dried it warped some but it was there to stay. There were four rooms at the beginning and the fifth added later. Bobby even made the doors with the cross pieces on them much like the "Little House on the Prairie" It was pretty crude, but it was our house and we were happy. We couldn't afford indoor plumbing, and Bobby made the outside privy and we hauled water from the neighbors well for a while. We both were full of energy and we did most everything that was done inside the house. We both worked on the kitchen cabinets, and I wallpapered with a pretty ivy pattern. It looked so pretty and bright to us. We were home improvement people by choice. Bobby found some hardwood flooring, and started putting it down in the kitchen. He only had a few hours at a time to work on it, so until it was finished, we walked on two levels of floor. The black paper on the outside of the house would protect it until we could put siding on it. I'm sure nobody admired our house like we did. It certainly wasn't ready for a house warming party. There wasn't much to keep the rats out, and every night when the "Big" rat arrived, it would sound like a saw mill cranking up. Bobby would hit on the wall, and it would get quite for a short time. But in the winter time we stayed warm as toast because Mr. Brown put a little flue in our bedroom for the heater. The only problem we had a leak or two. We didn't put a Bible in the corner of our house, but it was built on lots of prayers. We were living alright using the water sparingly, but soon we would need more water because our other two children would be born. Our little house sat proudly with our little one seated '39 Ford car in the yard. When Robert Steve was born at Minnie G Boswell Hospital, It was such a special occasion that Bobby borrowed his sister's two seated Oldsmobile to come and pick us up. I had bought a pattern and made him a layette. All babies wore dresses at that time regardless if it was a girl or boy. But I had a special bought dress for him to wear back home from the hospital. Now we were enjoying our new baby and our little new unfinished house. We put Steve's bed in our bedroom. Never would I have put him in another room even if I had one. There wasn't much spare time for me any more. The baby clothes and diapers had to be boiled on our bedroom heater. We didn't have a washing machine or a dryer but we had a clothes line outside. Pampers were not around at that time. Only imagine how many diapers were to be washed every day. In two years and seven months Steve would have a brother. He was Hiram Randall and we would call him Randy. He was a very good natured child, full of energy. I had to make new clothes for him too, but this time we had a washing machine and clothes dryer. What a blessing that was! Bobby had bought a peach of a car, a one owner maroon Ford. And this time he didn't have to borrow a car to pick us up at the hospital. Now our little family had grown as much as it would grow. Our boys had no boundary lines around our home to play. The angel of the Lord had to encamp around them. They enjoyed each others company and played good together. They had special pets that stayed close by them. Randy enjoyed just rolling on the ground with a dozen little puppies snagging his clothes. Steve always liked to improve and make things different than what they were. They had some friends that lived close by and two cousins that would spend a week with us most every summer. We had a pony named "Dixie" and she surprised us with a little colt. He was cute as could be with long legs and running with her with his tail straight up when we saw him. It was so full of energy and grew up along by her side. But soon the boys discovered it had a very bad habit of sneaking up behind you and biting.

"WATER RUSHING THROUGH THE PIPES"

By this time, we had to do more to our house. We put tile on the floor and I wallpapered the second bedroom. We needed a bath room, but we couldn't hire a plumber so Bobby got out the "Sears Roebuck" catalog, and placed an order for the outfit. He got his tools together and started digging trenches and a hole for the septic tank. In the middle of this, he had an appendix attack. He went to the doctor with the hurting not knowing he would have an emergency operation. But it didn't take long for the doctor to decide he needed the operation then. Now I was left with all the chores, the bathroom was not finished and I could hardly wait for the completion. As soon as he got back home, he started right back on the job. I wanted him to wait until he was healed better, but he was so anxious that he started right away. What a joy when the water started rushing through the pipes into our house! Now I could use all the water I wanted to. Surely we would never need anything else. The well had been dug. Now we didn't have to haul any more water. The dry sink had been instantly turned into a wet sink.

"MAILMAN CAME WITH A NOISY BOX"

We had heard on "Ernest Tubb's" radio show about some baby chicks for sale. That seemed to be a good thing raising some chickens to eat. So we put in an order. One day the mailman came and blew his horn. Oh boy! The baby chicks had arrived. They were mailed in a box will lots of holes in it. They were so pretty, little yellow fuzzy peeping chicks. Steve and Randy got real excited. They just had to touch them over and over. Bobby made a coup for them and but a light bulb inside to keep them warm for a few weeks, and the children enjoyed watching and feeding them. But soon the soft and cuddly fuzz wore off, and it was time to put them in the freezer. I would hang them up by their feet on the clothes line, and cut their heads off. That was a job I didn't enjoy doing and neither did the boys like to see it done, but it became necessary. We had plenty of chicken for our freezer now. Bobby was still working at the furniture company, but he had some calves and a pig. We felt like real farmers. Even though some mornings he would find a calf missing, and he would have to find it before he left for work. But he never complained about it.

"TRAGEDY STRIKES"

One afternoon two men came from the plant where Bobby was employed with some awful news. Bobby had been taken to a hospital in Athens. He had cut the cornea in his eye with a staple gun accident. I had never driven in a large town like Athens. But I got my sister, Mary and we found the hospital. Bobby was laying there with both eyes bandaged and sand bags on each side of his head, with instructions not to turn or lift his head. This went on for eleven days. The hospital had no recliners but straight chairs to sit in. That's where I sat each night for the length of his stay. Arrangements were made for the children to stay with mama and daddy. They had never stayed away from home at night before this time. I would only leave the hospital long enough for baths and clean clothes and to see the boys. The first time I went home to an empty house with the boys, it was over whelming, I just couldn't keep from crying. The house seemed so lonely and sad with a very heavy burden to bear. A nurse had told me that Bobby might never see again. We needed a big miracle. But during his stay in the hospital when he was hurting so bad, he recalls a time when God just poured an ointment seemingly over his eye and soothed the pain. The head of the family disabled, and the insurance stated that both eyes had to be blind before it would pay anything. No lawyer wanted to come against the company insurance. Working people were still being mistreated. The workman's compensation finally agreed to pay him thirty dollars a week for three years, After he was able to go back to work, he had to work under extreme hardships with a serious eye injury. The pain and recuperating with lots of adjusting of depth and nervousness was just too much for him. We realized we had to do something else. We made a budget that was very sacrificial. We turned the large broiler house into an upholstery shop, and that was the beginning of "Brown's Custom Furniture." Bobby left the furniture plant never to return again to another employer. He always had great patience and determination to make things work. So he came home smiling and with zeal to become a real entrepreneur and I was ready to sacrifice with him. I took a course in Interior Decoration so I could help customers with choosing fabrics and colors. After a year I had my diploma. I discovered I had a talent in that field and it would not be wasted because it would help me in our own home too. The business started coming in and we never had a slow time. That was another blessing in disguise.

"BOBBY'S FIRST INVENTION AND UPHOLSTERY"

A chiropractor doctor from Madison came by one day and looked around and asked Bobby if he could make a special adjusting table for him. Bobby never turned down an opportunity, so he said yes and started getting everything together that he would need. His first trip was to the "Farmall" tractor parts place. There he bought a throttle and springs, then some plywood. We ordered maroon vinyl from our material supplier and the adjusting table began to take shape. The doctor was really impressed with the finished product. He had orders from many chiropractors and would fill a truck and deliver them to individual offices. In retrospect he wonders why he didn't get it patented, but attaining a patent is very expensive and we did not have the money then. With Bobby's experience in fine furniture making, he started making some custom furniture. That and the re-upholstery were keeping him very busy. He had many satisfied customers that came back again and again. Now that our youngest son and his wife bought the business, some of the old customers still come back. The children liked the idea of having daddy close by, and since tacks were used the floor always had lots of tacks on it, but they could walk through bare footed and never get one in their feet. Sterilized tacks were used by filling the mouth with them and using a magnetic hammer to tack them on the upholstery, hence the name "spitting tacks." I wish now that I had kept one of the miniature sofas Randy made with pieces of scrap wood, scrap cotton and cloth with lots and lots of tacks. It would remind him of how far he has come, since he builds such nice furniture now. But that's wishful thinking. We needed a better building and had a concrete block building made. It really looked nice to us. We added on several times as more space was needed. We always put in regular hours plus extra too. We always tried to make that first impression a good one, and let the customer know that their furniture was well taken care of while it was in our possession. There were some funny things to remember about the upholstery days. One day he was called to a house to pick up a chair to be upholstered. It had been noised about that this house had lots of animals in it, but he did not expect to see a goat sitting in the chair he was to pick up, looking at television and chewing his cud. He liked his chair just the way it was. There was a pet pig there too, along with other pets. The hog lot he went through at another place didn't have the best entrance. There was a great big huffy hog and a pink ribbon on the gate. Guess she had some little piglets. But Bobby was always accommodating any place and any time.

"SCHOOL DAYS"

Time had come for Steve to start to school. It was hard to let him go. After I took him to his room, I stood in the hall with other parents that felt the same as I did. I didn't think anybody could take care of my children like I could. Before I left, I went back into the room. I saw a tear run down his cheek. I asked him what was wrong. He said something got in my eye. I wiped it off and pretended I believed him. After that time he was alright. Then I went home and started worrying. Would he go to the restroom when he needed to, would he go to the lunch room, would he get on the right bus to come home? All these things bothered me until I saw the bus coming. He hopped off like he was used to it. He was dressed in new clothes from top to bottom. So he changed clothes, had a snack and was ready to play with Randy. Two years later we would go through the same things with Randy going to school. We knew he would really like it. But we were very wrong. I really believed he wanted to go to school, but the big yellow bus always made his stomach hurt. He would go on to school, but it was a common practice that the nice bus driver Mr. Head would bring him back and say little Brown didn't want to stay at school today, so I brought him home. The teacher had thick magnified glasses, and I don't think he had ever seen anybody that looked like that. I often wondered if that was the reason he was frightened. But he and his daddy made some kind of deal unknown to me and finally he started liking school. He was always a good student.

"SOME PLAY TIMES"

Steve and Randy always played good together and since Steve was the oldest, he was the leader. One day they were out catching lizards and cutting their tails off. There were lots of leaves on the ground and Steve sent Randy back to the house to get something. As he ran his boot strings were loose, and they started flapping on his legs. He just knew it was those lizards, and he got hysterical. Bobby had to catch him and calm him down. They would play so much that Randy would always fall asleep at the supper table. They enjoyed the country living to the fullest. They didn't think of us as being poor, they just had some good times. One day Bobby took Dixie our pony to his sister's house so the cousins could ride in the pony cart. Bill had a pony too, But he didn't like to run fast (we thought). Everything was going well and they all were having fun when Bill's pony hooked to our cart decided to run away. Steve and Bill were in the cart. It was a nightmare. Our hearts started racing. It ran into the road in front of cars, we all were helpless. But for some reason it decided to turn and run back across the road into the yard. That was a blessing. It ran across a pipe in the yard and threw both boys out in a rose bush. They only got some scratches .We ran to see if they were alright, and decided then we would keep the cart at home thereafter.

"OUR VACATION TIMES"

My school class went to Daytona Beach, Florida on our senior trip. I remembered the beautiful beach and scenery, so as our family was able to go on a three day and night vacation, we went to Daytona. Steve was about six years old and Randy almost four. We were all excited, especially Steve. We were loading up our nice little Ford car and Steve got his toe hurt in the door. But the excitement didn't let him dwell on the pain. When we arrived at Daytona, we rode up the beach, the sun was shining and the waves were moving in so gracefully. It was so beautiful. We found some rooms on the beach front and walked down to the ocean before we un-packed. A nice breeze was blowing and we knew we were going to have a wonderful time. We didn't know the boys were both getting sore throats. The next morning we walked down to the beach and we found some little donkeys just waiting for some one to take pictures. We sat both of them on one and took some pictures and by then we could see they weren't feeling well. By night we could tell they were getting tonsillitis which both had so often. So we decided to leave a day early and see our Doctor Parker. But when we left, we knew that would be our vacation spot for years to come. Thereafter, we always stayed at family owned motels with kitchens so we could cook and eat which would save us money. We would stay in a place that had a coffee room right on the beach. That's where we got acquainted with "coffee mate" in small packages. One summer just a day before we would leave on our trip, I noticed a few bumps on Steve. I took him to the doctor to see what it was. He took a look at him and said it could be chicken pox, but that might be all that he will break out. Go ahead the salt water will be good for him. That was good news to us because we wanted to go so bad. We packed that night and left before day light. The children were still sleeping but just before we got to Daytona they started waking up and poor Steve was breaking out all over. We had little choice as what to do. We just went on and tried not to look so guilty. But we could hear whispers when we would pass others saying he's got chicken pox. Steve had a good time anyway, but the itching really got bad. We bought calamine lotion and by the time we left, he was almost plastered in it. That year the pictures were not good. Steve was just pitiful looking. After we got home Randy had them too, but being at home we could deal with them much better than being on vacation. But the memories we had of Daytona Beach still lingers on.

"THE DRIVE-IN RESTAURANT"

This was a favorite place for us at least once a week. It was not far from home, but we cleaned up like we were going to a far away fancy restaurant. The boys looked forward to getting the hamburgers with a pickle and coke, and when they saw the waiter coming to our car with the order, they would really get excited. The window would be rolled down, and the tray slid over the door. This was their weekly treat. We never cooked hamburgers at home, but we always had three meals a day. They were breakfast, dinner and supper. We all ate at the same time and never left the table with food in our hands. The time at the table was always a special time for us to be together. I tell my grandchildren that what they call lunch is really dinner because when we were on the farm, mama always had to ring the big black dinner bell at twelve o'clock for the farm workers to stop and eat. Again at one o'clock to go back to work. But that's another thing that has been changed in the pass few years.

"SURGERY FOR THE BOYS"

Steve had to miss so many days at school his first year due to tonsillitis, so we decided it would be good to have both boys tonsils removed at the same time. This would be done before school started again. Minnie G Boswell hospital was close by and we would have both in the same room. Bobby could look after one and I would look after the other. So we had them admitted and waited for the surgery to be over. The idea sounded good until Randy was brought back and a little blood was coming from his mouth. I was at Steve's bed and both the Doctor and I saw Bobby sliding down the wall. He was told to put his head between his legs. He was just about ready to faint. At that point it looked like I would have two patients and a husband to care for, but Bobby recovered shortly. They both did fine, and gifts started coming in for them and they got pretty noisy. Their aunt Mary sent them a monkey on a string that reached from one bed to the other, and that really caused a stir. They had so much fun with that, we were afraid they were using their throats too much, and they might start bleeding but that never happened. We were beginning to wonder if we would be put out of the hospital if they didn't calm down. That was an operation that really helped them, and they never had to miss school again with sore throats.

"REAL EXPLORERS"

Every where Steve and Randy went chubby, their dog was always with them, he was a real pal. If I missed the boys and called chubby he would always show up, then I would know where they were. They rambled through all the woods and fields exploring everything. One day Steve found a dead bird on the ground. He dug a hole to bury it and asked me if birds went to heaven. When I told him only people went to heaven, he was real upset. One day they came running in the house announcing "We have found a watermelon tree" and they had the proof in their hands. It turned out to be a sassafras bush. And it did smell like watermelon. It could have been very convincing. Another time they came in out of breath from running so fast. They could hardly talk, but they had found some sink holes in the woods, which were in line and after looking over the area good, they realized it was a cemetery. We didn't know there was a cemetery in that area, so we thought that needed to be investigated further and afterwards we learned it was a slave cemetery. So the boys avoided that spot from then on. I had two nephews, Bill and Warren that would come down every summer for a week, they had always lived in the city, and they loved to be with us. They were like two birds out of a cage. With four boys all about the same age getting in to so much would sometimes get on my nerves, but we were always entertained at the end of their vacation with a play. It was always cowboys and Indians. And the left over garden crop of squash and may-pops were always good weapons for the plays. They would gather a large crowd of friends around to come and sit in the yard to watch the act. It was pretty professional like. They did all the planning and it didn't cost us any money. But when the cousins left it didn't stop our boys from getting into mischief. Steve and Randy were always playing jokes on their grandpa Moon. They would sneak around looking at everything. They had noticed a jar of Vaseline in the privy and assumed he was using it for some medicinal purpose. They found a jar of Mentholatum and mixed a little of it in with the Vaseline and kept watch for his next trip in. They knew when he would come out he would be furious, so they got a little pole and laid it across the door. They watched afar off. They never admitted that to him, but he knew they were the culprits that did it.

"A BRAND NEW CAR"

Our work was paying off and Bobby wanted a new car. He had seen a fifty eight Ford on display at the Ben Thompson's Ford Co. in Madison. It was a two tone beige color deluxe car. I was told it had a great big engine, and it must have because so many times we would be going somewhere just minding our own business when a patrol would drive up. "Speeding ticket" It ran so smooth, we didn't realize it was going as fast as it was. But now he knew he could pay for it and he traded his car in and drove it in our driveway with a big smile on his face. "Finally we were beginning to move up the ladder." We made several trips to Florida for our vacations, and some short trips to the north Georgia Mountains. But with the experience Bobby had as a child in the mountains, he never cared to go back. He never wanted to stay a whole week there. But we really did enjoy that car. After the boys were married, we didn't enjoy going to the beach as much, because we really went so they could have a good time.

"WE NEEDED A NEW HOUSE"

We needed a loan to build a house so we went to a bank that we had never borrowed money from and got a loan. All the years we had been married, we never spent money on anything else until we got our bills paid, so we had built a good credit rating. Mr. Griffin the president told Bobby to start building the house and write checks until it was completed and then the loan would be made. We used that bank for many years and will always be grateful to him for trusting in us. We got the best quality for the best prices. The contractors started in January and the work was slow with a full basement being dug, and heavy beams that was brought in on big trucks. January was a rainy month too, and there was plenty red mud to contend with. The rocks were brought in from Apple Valley Tennessee for our large chimney. Finally every thing was finished but the painting, and Bobby and I took over and did most of the inside painting. Some nights we would paint until one and two o'clock. The boys would sometimes get in the new bath tubs and go to sleep. This time quality furniture was purchased that will never be replaced. God had blessed us again. Even with effects lingering on from the depression, we paid every payment on time. This time our two car garage was graced with a new '66 Ford car with air condition!

"STEVE AND HIS MANY TALENTS"

Steve was always interested in drawing for school functions, especially for the ball games. He would have several teens come over and he would stretch out a long banner on the floor and sketch off the slogans for the Bulldog ball team at school. They all would help fill in with magic markers. This was preparing him for his later business of commercial art. He learned to play a guitar early and started getting some of his friends over to practice for a band in our basement. The drums would vibrate so loud, we didn't encourage that at all. But later on Steve joined a gospel group playing his bass guitar and he and the young part of the group made a recording. They received several recognitions. At other times, Steve and Randy could think up some of the funniest things to do. One day they decided Steve would call some people we knew and tell them to cover their phones with a paper bag. He was going to blow them out and that would keep dust from filling the house. Randy would be on another phone and listen. One person was trying to put the bag over the phone and it started to tear, they said hold it just a minute let me get another bag. Nobody caught Steve's voice and he could do it without getting tickled. He had lots of people agreeing with him that the phones got better after the cleaning job. A preacher we knew well asked us the next day if ours was cleaned out too. Then Steve told him it was a prank. Nobody got mad but laughed at it. At the age of fifteen, we bought him his first car, and he was only allowed to drive it with Bobby or me with him for the first year. This gave him a year of experience before he was turned loose in the big world with freedom he would not know how to handle. He obeyed us and when he was sixteen, he was allowed his freedom even though sometimes we would have to put some restraints on him. He liked to skip school and get some friends to ride some with him. One times he even went to South Carolina to pick up some fireworks. After high school, we enrolled him in Lee College in Tennessee. He stayed for one semester and didn't like it at all. He was bored so much he said. One day he called and wanted to come back home he had not been feeling well, so we told him he could come. It wasn't long afterwards that he married and started his own business and named it "Brown Art Signs" That ended his college days.

"STEVE GETS MARRIED"

Steve married Beverly and after about six years, they gave us our first grandson. He was Robert Wesley. Beverly and Steve were so excited when time came for them to go to the hospital. Beverly couldn't fine her house coat, so I loaned her one of mine to wear. We drove them to Athens. The weather was mild in November and Steve went without a coat. But by morning, the weather turned bitter cold. It was a long wait for Wesley to be born, but finally the nurse came down the hall with Wesley wrapped all up for us to see. About six years later, they gave us another son, this time it was James Christopher. The wait was not as long this time, but we had to care for Wesley while they were in the hospital, and he felt a little jealous. After he saw his little brother the next day he cried most of the way home with us. Chris had black hair when he was born, and all Wesley could think of was I wanted a brother with white hair like mine.

"RANDY GETS A NEW CAR"

Randy became fifteen and it was time to get him a car. He was very hard to please we thought, but he knew what he wanted and was not satisfied with the same kind we got for Steve. When Bobby would suggest one, Randy would make fun of it. It would either be so big it echoed, or the tires would look like bicycle tires. After he looked for a long time, he saw just the right car. It was a "Mach 1" Ford Mustang. Red with white interior with the extras he wanted. He was very proud of it and never abused it any way. He was treated the same as Steve, no driving without Bobby or me until he was sixteen. After high school, he chose to go to Athens Tech. After his technical school, he started to work and later married Angie. They bought the little house that Randy's grandparents had lived in for many years. Randy was very independent, but Bobby helped him a lot on repairing the house. After about five years they gave us a little grand daughter, Elizabeth Anne and would call her Libby. They didn't ask us to go to the hospital with them, but when they said they were ready to go, they waited longer than we thought they should. They were about forty five minutes from the hospital. And they barely made it. It was a bitter cold night in January but we went on to the hospital to see our first little girl that was born into our family. The next child they had was Amanda Jean. She was born in May, when flowers were in bloom. Which I think fits her personality. And the last one was a boy, named after both grandparents. He was Robert Dewey and would be called Rob. He was the Christmas baby. We have been blessed with five special grandchildren and we wouldn't trade them with anybody.

"HORSES FOR WESLEY AND LIBBY"

Bobby never had a horse when he was a child, so he thought Libby and Wesley would like to have one. That would be their Christmas present. Wesley's was Patches, and Libby's was Saucy Sue. When they were brought to our pasture, Saucy Sue did not like the trailer and had gotten scraped up pretty bad. She had to be doctored on for a while. Patches made the trip alright. When they got the right age to be trained we sent them to a trainer, and we bought all the proper gear for them. When they were brought back to our pasture they were fine, but Patches was a little too spirited for most people and he would run wide open. They both were quarter horses. People were having problems staying on him. Wesley rode him a little, but never really liked him. He finally sold patches and used the money for his college expense. Saucy Sue had a leg injury later and Libby was her vet for a long time, but she finally died. Libby loved all the animals and they would react to her love. When I was young, I loved to ride horses but as I got older, realizing the danger of broken bones, I stopped riding them because I didn't want to be in a cast.

PART 3:

"BOBBY'S MEMORIES OF LIFE IN NORTH GA"

"BOBBY'S MEMORIES OF THE 30's" AND FAMILY LIVES

He remembers his life as almost un-believable, especially in America. The person that knew privation for years during the depression would grow up to be prosperous in so many ways. His life certainly did not start that way. When he was about three years old, and lived in Maysville, Georgia, his family always lived on farms as a share cropper. During the thirty's, life was very hard on big families living in the rural areas, and living on farms owned by the rich. His mommy always had faith in God and always expected better times. She had been raised in the mountains and knew how to survive even in hard times. He remembers one afternoon his daddy hooked up the mule to the wagon, and took the family to a Pentecostal meeting. Mom was a Pentecostal, and daddy didn't have much on his mine except some week end drinking and farming. He would take the family to the meetings. Some times it was brush arbor meetings. That particular night I went to sleep on the ground, and I was awakened by a big commotion. People were hollering and running and scared half to death. The reason was one man had a T Model Ford car, and he cranked it in gear. The car was coming back into the brush arbor. After much ado, the car ran into a post and was stopped. After all of the frustration, they found out no body was hurt, so all the parents got the families rounded up and put back in the wagons. Something had been proven then and there, they had the best mode of travel. Those automated vehicles were too fast, and un-predictable. Then there was the long journey back home. At that time, there were four girls, and three boys. My hair was snow white, and it was said, I was hard to find in a white cotton patch. I had never had a hair cut, I really liked my long curly hair, but mommy's idea was different, she wanted her boys to have short hair. So she placed me in a chair and my oldest sister "Georgie" got the scissors. I cried, but my tears didn't stop the haircut. I sat there and watched the little curls fall to the floor. But time healed all the hurts, and I got over it.

"TIMES WERE VERY HARD"

In the fall of one year, there was evidence of a very bad year. Daddy was working as a share cropper, and when time came to settle up, there was nothing. And I remember hearing enough to let me know that there was no money and the groceries had run out. There were eight children at that time to feed, and mommy and daddy. And the time looked dark. Daddy had to get out and see if he could get some other work. I remember there was a WPA. I didn't know what that meant, but I knew it was a long way off. And we had no car. I learned later that President Roosevelt had these places set up to help the people survive. Jefferson, Georgia was the place he would have to go. I don't know the exact miles that he had to walk, because we children never got to go to town, only daddy went to look after the business, and to buy the groceries. The salary was going to be a minimum wage, but that was better than nothing. He would leave home before day light and get back at night, so late we would all be asleep. Mama would fix whatever she could find for him to take for his lunch. We had more cornbread than any thing else. I remember weeks when we never saw daddy during this time. Winter was coming on, and we didn't have shoes to wear. Daddy had to measure my foot so he could pick up a pair of shoes in Jefferson for me. The only thing he had to measure them with was a straw. He put the straw in his pocket, and somehow, the straw must have broken on the trip. The shoes that he bought for me was too little, but when they asked me if they fit, I said yes they fit. And I wore them until they rubbed blisters on my feet. I knew if I didn't keep them that would be my only chance for shoes that year. After I finally took them off, my feet were so sore I couldn't get them back on. Well, my feet were tough, I'd make it somehow, but it was a cold "Winter without Shoes"

"MY SHOES WERE SWAPPED FOR A SIDE OF PORK"

The next thing I remembered was somebody telling daddy about work being available in Morgan County. This must be the Land of milk and honey, people that we knew had been there and were able to get jobs and support their families better. Daddy got down there and was given a job. There he got a job working by the day. The landlady sent a truck back to pick up our earthly possessions, and the family. It took more room for the family than it did for our possessions. All of the old straw was removed from the mattress ticks and only the ticks were rolled up and brought along. So when we got to Morgan County I remember the clean smell of new straw in our mattress tick. It was beginning to get cold and we had some friends that were in the same financial condition that we were in. They had a large family too. Many people from the mountains had moved down to Morgan County soon as they could. That was a very cold winter, and the prettiest snow I had ever seen. My feet would almost freeze, but I would just have to make a quick run out in it every now and then. When you don't have shoes, you really like summer weather. There were lots of children on the farm so we played and had lots of fun even though we all were poor. I still had my shoes that were too small, and the other family had a child that my shoes would fit. They didn't have any money but they had a "Side of Pork Meat" So a swap was made. That meant I had to spend the rest of the winter without shoes. A very cold "Winter without Shoes."

"THE WASH HOLE"

There were about six families on the farm and all the women would get together and make a wash area, we called the wash hole. All the families lived on the same level, so there was no "Jones" to keep up with. They would make their soaps, and boil clothes in the pot to get them clean. We had floors with big cracks in them but the shuck mops mommy made and the lye soap she used made the floors smell so clean. The wash hole was a good play ground. All the children would pull limbs out of trees to put around the pot to get a real hot fire going. The water would be boiling There was a big flat rock, and we had a battling stick cut out of a piece of wood. One side would be flat. This stick was used to dip the clothes out of the boiling water and battled or hit on the flat rock. This would beat all of the dirt loose. Who said we needed an agitator, or exercise class? It would take all day to get the washing done. Then they would hang them on lines, on bushes or anywhere there was room to dry. Another day of the week was ironing day. The old black irons were heated on a wood stove or fireplace to iron over the rough clothes. If it was a hot day, you just sweated more. At this time our clothes were made out of the fertilizer sacks and flour sacks. I remember seeing mommy dye fertilizer cloth with red clay to make a colored cloth. It wasn't long before daddy wanted to sharecrop again, so we moved away to another farm. The sharecropper gave daddy some allowance to live on, which was ten dollars a month. By that time there was another one in the family. So that was a dollar for each. Daddy would pay this back with seed money. You can believe there was no extra money. Our grocery list would consist of salt, pepper, soda, flour and snuff. Just the bare necessities were bought. I remember one time when our clothes got down to no changing suits. When wash day came, I would have to stay in the house. If anybody came, I found a door to get behind. Hopefully nobody would come. We had so little, but mommy never got discouraged. She always looked for a better day.

"OUR LIVES AT HOME"

Mommy knew exactly when to hunt for the seasonal wild foods that God supplied. She had been raised in the mountains and her great grandmamma was a Cherokee Indian. We would go out and hunt berries, poke salet and creeses when the right season came. When these started cooking, we could hardly wait to eat. There were no fancy dishes for our table. Hopefully, there would be enough syrup can lids that everybody could have one for a plate. When we moved, there would always be syrup to bring. We always managed to keep a milk cow. Even though she was a faithful cow, she couldn't give enough milk for the family. I guess we were some of the first people that had two percent milk. We had no way of keeping anything cool, except to lower it into the well in the bucket. Our evening meal was always two percent milk and cornbread. Ruth would always cook the cornbread for supper when mommy was in the field, since she was the oldest one at home after Georgie got married. We could smell it cooking before we got into the house. She always looked after the little ones at home too. Mommy always had a good garden during the late spring and summer. We would have sweet potatoes to be hilled for winter. These were usually cooked at dinner time. We didn't have enough eating utensils so you might end up with a spoon or fork. We had a handmade table with benches if you didn't get there on the first call, you had to stand and eat. No one had to be called the second time. Neither did we ever complain about what we had to eat. Mommy would sew and make clothes when she collected enough sacks. Daddy did all the plowing with a mule. After the garden was over we would have dried peas to thrash. They would be put in a burlap sack and hung on the clothes line. They would be beaten with a stick until the hulls came to the top and then emptied out. That would leave the peas clean. When peas would be on the menu for the next day, some would be put in a pan of water at night to soak for the meal the next day. My older brother, Winfred liked to hunt and he always had a way of slipping off to go hunting. He liked to do anything but work. He would take me with him to his rabbit boxes and fishing sometimes. He made the rabbit boxes just right to catch those rabbits. They could be swapped for other things or sold for a little money. One time he had me to hold a rabbit until he went to another box. I was holding it the best I could but it jumped out of my hand. I was so afraid of telling him I had lost it, but I went to the next box, and there was a rabbit in it. Now I didn't have to tell him I lost the one he had entrusted me with. He made a flip that would kill a rabbit as good as a gun would. He would hunt the woods until he found just the right forked stick. That would make the ideal flip. Of course, he didn't know what the word dynamics was. One day I went to his rabbit boxes with him and the first one had a rabbit in it, so he told me to stay with it so nobody could come by and get it. I was staying close by and low and behold I looked up and a black man was coming down the field. That was the first black person I had ever seen. It liked to have scared me to death. I lay flat as I could on the ground hoping he wouldn't see me and sure enough he went on by without seeing me. I had seen lots of strange things but this one caused me to really wonder. One day something scary looking was on one of Winfrred's set hooks in the creek. It was my first time to see an eel. But he took it home and filled a dishpan with it. He would put me on his back when crossing a creek so I would not get wet. When it had rained and too wet to work in the fields, I would go fishing with mommy. She loved to fish, but she didn't like to clean them. That always was daddy's job. Ezra liked to get his dogs together and go possum hunting. I don't remember what he would do with them but I don't remember ever eating any. He was pretty small but he would fight you in a minute. One day he whipped a boy at school pretty bad because the boy called him a bad name. Mommy always taught us not to use bad language. And he was not about to let him call him a bad name. Faye did not like to go to the fields. She liked to keep the house in order. She was always re-arranging our furniture. The bed might be in a different place when you started to get in it. But Hattie always bossed us around and we thought she ought to be a lawyer or preacher one. She always wanted to tell each of us what we needed to do. We always had chores to do and we did them without a fuss. Phoebe, David and Hazel were the youngest ones and I married without knowing much about their lives at home. The landlord would give us five cents for every snuff box of boll weevils we picked up during the time of the "Boll Weevils." I remember well the day I got my nickel and they let me go to the near by store. I pulled a cold drink out of the box and got a pack of soda crackers, and I was feeling big. That was a real treat for me. The landlords were the only ones that could have a nice meal and keep the whole house warm in the winter. We had to sit right around the fireplace in one room. I see the big churches now and the mansions, the big courthouses and big houses that were built back in that era, and I wonder where were these people when we were hungry and had so little.

"TIME FOR SCHOOL"

Daddy was looking for a good pay off at the end of one crop year. We had been kept out of school until the crops were gathered, and it was time to return to school. There were a few necessities needed. When the settlement was made, Daddy came home with forty dollars left. This was the best year yet. So the next day, we all got to go to town and each one got a new school outfit. We had lots of corn, so daddy swapped some corn for a used car. The man told him it was a good car, but daddy did not know how to drive, and believed him. My oldest brother was old enough to drive, so they got the car. It was a long Chrysler convertible. It was out of gas, so they hooked it to the wagon and pulled it home. The next time they went to town, they bought a gallon of gas, and a tire for the car. They struggled trying to get the old tire off the wood spoke wheels. They couldn't decide how to get it off, so they made a fire, and burned the tire off the rim, keeping the rim wet so it wouldn't burn. They got the tire on the rim then, and put the gas in it. Pushing it down the road it would crank just for a while, and then it was all to do over. Finally they decided the car was no good. And it was swapped for a one seated car. (there were only ten of us now, and a one seated car.) School time came and we had to walk to school. Sometimes the teacher would meet us at a point, and take us on to school. If I had to sit in the front seat, I would put my hands over the holes in my pants knees to hide them from her. In the afternoons, we would have to walk all the way home. The Brownwood school had seven grades in one room. A pot bellied stove was in the room and a pot of soup would cook all morning. By dinner time it would smell so good.

If you had a nickel, you could get a bowl of soup. If not you would have to go outside. I never had the nickel so I would eat my cornbread and syrup or the like on the outside.

"POLITICAL RALLEY"

My Grandpa Brown was a fan of "Gene Talmadge," and he got daddy and Winfred to take him to one of his rallies when he was running for Governor. We had acquired a nice 1935 Plymouth car at that time. He was sitting on the back seat of the car just looking the car over and testing everything out, when he accidently pulled the door handle. The doors opened from front to back on this car. The door flew open and almost sucked him out of it. That was a bad design for the Plymouth. But he enjoyed going to see Talmadge. One of his lines was "The poor dirt farmer ain't got but three friends on this earth. They are God Almighty, Sears Roebuck and Gene Talmadge." My great grandpa married one of the Patton girls from the bowl shaped valley of the lower "Cartoogechaye" creek out from Franklin,North Carolina known as "Patton Valley." She was a descendent of George Patton. The Pattons were large land owners, but when the depression hit they were hurt too. Some of them left the valley and moved elsewhere. But Patton Valley is still a land mark. One of the Patton kin married Davy Crockett. He had only about six months of school, and served honorable as a member of Congress of the United States and in the Tennessee legislature. Davy went far in his day by his own effort and achievements and was high in the esteem of his fellow men. But education was taught among the Pattons and most of them got very highly recognized for it and some sat in very prominent places in government.

"TOY MAKING"

We made most of our toys. I remember how we made a "Flying Jenny." We found a good tree stump. Then we got a metal peg and heated it until we got a good size hole burned in the stump. We cut a tree that was straight, and centered it so we could burn another hole in it to fit over the peg. We found some axle grease and filled the hole, and greased the entire top of the stump. That would really speed it up. Then we placed the peg in the hole and the tree on the stump. One would hang on to each end, while one stood at the stump and pushed until it got up good speed. It had the right name it was a "flying" jenny. The person pushing would pick a good time to run out from in the circle without getting hit. I think of how dangerous it was, but how much fun we had too. With a bunch of brothers and sisters you could really get in to lots of trouble. One day a corn stalk cutter was setting in the field with the cutter arm locked in place. Faye played with me lots since she was the next age up. Ezra was younger, but would always be around. We were playing on the stalk cutter moving all the parts and by an accident somebody released the arm and it fell right on top of Ezra's head. We were in trouble now. It started bleeding and mommy had taught us not to tell stories, so we thought things over and decided we had better just hide behind the barn with him for a while, it was a chance it might stop bleeding and we wouldn't have to tell. But time went on and the bleeding didn't stop, so we had to take him to mommy and take the punishment. After she doctored on him he healed up. When we decided to make another toy small trees stood a chance of being used. We decided to make us a wagon. Well we got busy and found a good round tree and sawed off some wheels. Again we heated a metal peg and burned holes in each wheel to attach a carved axle. We made a pretty good body and attached a handle. It was a good fair weather wagon, because if it rained mud would stick to the wheels, and it was too heavy to pull.

The Ervin family lived near us and one of the boys named Grady made a toy from a metal wheel from a old wagon wheel hub. He made a hook on the end of a piece of wire and we could always hear him coming to our house. He could make lots of sounds with the wheel and we loved that idea, so we all started getting the old wagon hubs and making us a toy like that. Mommy's daddy built some of the furniture for the "Weatherly" house at Dillard, Ga. which is the "York" house now. So we had inherited some talent to build things from both sides of our family. At the end of the days, mommy would read more from the "Robinson Crusoe" book to us.

"MY FIRST SEX LESSON"

Our one room school had all classes in it. A time of activity was issued to each class. The teacher gave my class time to go to the chalk board and draw. I had never had chalk before and I thought I would draw a little boy's picture. I knew more about little boys than anything else. As I was drawing, I heard some snickering going on and I thought they must really like my drawing. About that time the teacher came over and grabbed the eraser from my hand and erased it off the board and told me to go sit down. I didn't understand why she did that, neither did I know that it was wrong to draw a little boy without clothes on. I learned a lesson too that day. Now I know why I would always hide behind the door when I was waiting for clean clothes to put on. Many years passed and the teacher asked me to bring my guitar to school and play for the class during the devotion time. I guess she forgot I never got a bowl of soup there. But that was a thrill for me and I proudly took my guitar. Later on in the "Buckhead" school, my teacher there asked me to bring my guitar too. Some of the boys there started getting guitars and wanted me to learn them some chords. And that thrilled me to do it.

"A PET PIG"

We had a little pig given to us. We made it a little bed beside the fireplace and it was so tiny, mommy fed it with an eye dropper. It would follow us around like a puppy. When people would come up, it would make a noise that let us know someone was around. But soon it forgot about the kindness we had shown to it, and he got mean, attacking people. One day we were picking blackberries and he tried to bite me. We would have to carry a stick around to protect our selves as well, until daddy put him up and we never knew what happened thereafter, but I suppose we ate him. Keeping the little pig warm reminded me of how my grandmamma would warm my feet when I went to see her at night in the cold weather. Before I would leave, she always heated the black iron in the fireplace and wrapped it in a towel, to cover up my feet. I was always her pet too. I was named after my grandpa Brown. I learned lots of things by watching him. He never smoked but he always raised some tobacco and hung it in the barn. He raised some of the biggest watermelons called "Stone Mountain." Now I can raise some just like him. But no one was allowed in his patch. He knew how to have a good garden.

"PLANT JOBS HELPED OUR FAMILY"

As the family got older, some of my sisters got jobs in sewing plants in Madison. My daddy got a better job overseeing a farm in Morgan County. He was converted, and never drank any more. But before when he had been drinking, Mama could tell it when she would see him walking from the store. He always set his hat on his head different. He knew she was about to really jump on him, and he didn't want his eyes to show. It was a much better environment in our house when the drinking stopped. We had a nice big house with upstairs. Floors were nice and smooth. We had plastered walls and plenty of rooms. At this farm the "Andrews" lived across the road from us. This is when I met Benny and Raymond Andrews. Benny was always drawing things. And in one of Raymond's books he noted the "Browns" as being good white folks. There were twenty five mules for the farm and plenty of barns. My job was to take care of the mules and do some plowing. You can't imagine the amount of water a mule can drink until you have to draw the water. We enjoyed living in such a nice place. My sisters that were old enough got jobs at the sewing plant, and our eating habits changed a good bit, now we knew what loaf bread and mayonnaise was. We could have sandwiches to eat. We were getting in better financial shape with daddy making more money and the girls bringing in checks every week too. We could have nice clothes to wear. Later the mules were replaced with tractors, and that really pleased me. I loved to drive the tractor. I quit school, since I had not really had the opportunity to go like I should have. But the experiences I had, taught me so much about real life. I was determined to learn something new every day. Even though I didn't have any special education, God gave me wisdom and knowledge that only a few people ever attain. I could repair most any thing that wasn't working. Now I could get a factory job too and make some money. It was easy for me to learn a new job, and at the factory I was making fifteen dollars a week. I could buy all the clothes I wanted. Several of us liked music, and my oldest brother got me into a band with him. We played for street dances, and had a program on the radio. We were having lots of fun with our band and getting more appointments by being on the Athens radio station. I was known as "Curly" because of my curly hair. I could play most any instrument. We were feeling very important performing on stage.

We had six musicians. Winfred was the comedian, Ted West played rhythm guitar, Grover Ervin played guitar, Pop Peters played the fiddle, Ralph Sims played the wash board, and Bobby played the mandolin, guitar and sometimes the fiddle. Annie Sue Sims was the vocalist. Sometimes Bobby and Winfred would sing a duet. We just knew we would end up at "Nashville." But one night on our way home, we almost had a bad accident and I realized I didn't need to keep company with some of those boys. At home that night, I prayed that God would bring the right girl into my life, and I told him I was going to live for him. So as God always does, in a few weeks I was in Madison in a ten cents store, when I saw the girl that I knew God had sent to me. She was a tall blonde, and I thought she was the most beautiful girl in the whole world. She was real smart in school and in home economics had learned how to cook and I was so happy that I had found her. I asked her for a date, and soon within months, we were engaged to be married, and married shortly. Within that first year, we went to a Pentecostal revival and we both were born again. That made our lives together start off right.

"PROPHECY GIVEN TO BOBBY"

A CFO meeting was being held at Rock Eagle 4H center in Eatonton, which was close to our house. Bobby and I went all that we could. And we enjoyed the services so much. We met some very nice people that would make long time friends. At that time we had some property to sell, and a couple we met wanted to buy it. They loved our area, and would come by as much as they could. It was Jim that told Bobby about a mattress factory to be sold in Florida. Bobby got real excited, because at that time we were having the "Full Gospel Businessmen's Fellowship" meeting in our area where Bobby was vice president. A prophecy was given to Bobby about a new business venture. And Bobby felt sure this was the business, so he said I will buy it. He and our two boys went to Florida and moved the factory equipment here to Morgan County. Bobby had everything set up in his mind but we felt like we needed a professional to advise us some too, so we called a mattress consultant in to tell us what we needed to start the business. Soon we had it going. It was a slow growth, but we survived even though the interest rates soared to nineteen and half percent. This was the year nineteen eighty. Bobby had met Mr. Dudley Horton at a prayer breakfast, and knew he owned the "Horton Homes" factory so he met him one day and asked if he would buy some of our mattresses. Right away he introduced Bobby to his purchasing men and shortly we were making mattresses for them. That lasted for several years. We appreciated Dudley's kindness in trusting us to make mattresses for him. After years in the business, Bobby had an idea for a mattress set that was better than the ones we had seen in furniture stores and talking to customers we found out what they really wanted and we needed to get this idea patented. Bobby was so busy with the factory, he asked me to get that done. So we hired a patent attorney which meant lots of work on my part and lots of money. I had to talk to lawyers so much I got pretty educated in patent law. By nineteen eighty eight, we finally got the patent and trade mark for "The CUDDLER ENSEMBLE," in the United States and Canada. We named our business "Georgia Sleep Shops" which was incorporated. We both were very excited the day our lawyer called with the good news of the patent. Since the mattress business was growing, we both had about all we could handle. Several of the larger mattress companies liked our idea, but did not want to pay us royalties. We soon found that "Simmons" was infringing on our patented idea in Canada. Our lawyers had to handle that too. We had reporters coming out to take pictures of us on our mattress, and all the publicity was good. Bobby was listed in the "Who's Who of American inventors" book of 1990. But with Bobby's busy schedule he always had time to do other things. He was recognized for being a cooperative weather observer for 25 years with the weather bureau.

"A PRAYER GROUP BEGAN"

We wanted to have a prayer group in our home and six of us got together from different denominations. In just a few weeks many people were coming and many churches were represented here. We all looked forward to our Tuesday night prayer times. We called our basement room the "Upper Room." We would have testimonies, prayer and bible reading and just enjoy the fellowship. After several years, the opportunity arose that we could have a "Full Gospel Businessmen's Fellowship" in our area. We rented the banquet room at the Holiday Inn in Madison, and had Saturday morning breakfast each month. All of our prayer group would be there. Business men would invite others and their wives. There were business men from all kinds of businesses there. I played the piano for the praise service. At Christmas time one year, we invited the whole group to our home. We had the large basement room that was ideal for a large group. Even thought the weather was terribly cold, the house was packed. Bobby made such a big fire in the fireplace until people were playing musical chairs, trying to stay away from the heat. We have had so many good memories in our life, they are too numerous to mention. Our basement was used for so many good meetings. When somebody got sick, we would go and pray for them. Bobby recalls when Rudy and Maude Hicks and Joe Ashurst came to our house and had prayer for him when he had a broken leg. We were all about our "Father's Business." The man that wrote the "Dake Bible" which was Finis Dake was a speaker one night for us. We had lots of well known people to visit with us and give us their testimonies.

Years after that the dread name, cancer almost took my life in 1995, but I had a supernatural healing.

"FALL VACATIONS"

Since the children married and had families of their own, we changed our vacation time. We would go to the north Ga. Mountains for several nights with my sister Christine and her husband Watson, or go to St. Simons and Sea Island with another sister Mary and her husband Harry. Sea Island is a rich person's world, and we didn't have much in common there, but Mary liked to rent a large house and then invite us to come down and stay with them. We always enjoyed the time there, but I always envisioned having a small cottage close to the beach where I could just read and paint pictures, which are two hobbies of mine. We always enjoyed St. Simon's island too. Just to sit by the ocean and watch the big ships come by with the birds following close by knowing they would get some food. And just to hear the waves breaking against the large rocks. And to know that God was keeping that big body of water in it's rightful place. We also liked to go to Myrtle Beach and see all of the shows and visit all of the nice restaurants there.

"A TRIP BACK TO THE MOUNTAINS"

After Bobby's mother and daddy died, we had a van and we loaded it up with some of Bobby's sisters and headed to the mountains to reminisce. Hattie, Ruth, and Faye went with us. We started at Maysville, Ga. We went down a little dirt road over creeks and rivers to find some of the old home places. Finally after not recognizing the place, we came to a little country store. We were all thirsty so maybe we could get something to drink, and find the places we were looking for. Mr. Marlow the owner of the store we learned was sitting in a straight chair by the side door and called out, come on in. Well we went on in and got some little cokes from his cooler, which was not very cool. But we drank them any way. The store was typical of the mountain stores. It had a pot bellied stove and a wood floor that was worn from so much traffic. There was a bench on either side where the neighbors came and sat. After we had been there a short time some men started coming in to sit, they probably wanted to see who the strangers were. When they were asked what they wanted each of them would say, we're just checking in. Bobby told me later that he saw a little mouse playing around on the floor, I am so glad I didn't see that. Our visit would have been cut short. Someone had shucked corn, and a box of shucks was under the porch. A little bit of anything you wanted was in that little county store. Mr. Marlow's name was carved on each bench. After he found out we were friendly and had known some of the same people he did, we got some good information from him. Hattie started telling him things about the places we were hunting. She told him about the time a relative wrote to them at Maysville on a brown paper bag to come on down to Morgan county, money was growing on trees. They were picking peaches and were making a better living. Bobby joined in asking Mr. Marlow questions, and he seemed to be an authority on each of them. He knew all the places and all the people that had moved from there. And needless to say, it was a good stop. His directions were good, and after a while excitement swelled in the van. There's the "apple tree" Bobby couldn't believe apple trees lived that long. Then there's the "thorn tree" undoubtedly they all had been stuck on that one. They had discovered the old home place even though the house was not there. But it brought back many memories. It's amazing how even bad happenings bring back good memories. Then they thought about all of the people that had lived around them. All of them started revealing their memories. Many of the houses around were still in pretty good shape, although they couldn't find the one they had lived in. I looked at my watch, and it was getting close to five o'clock, and we had planned to spend the night in Dillard, Ga., so we went across a river on a wooden bridge that had been maintained and they all declared they had walked across it many a time. It was a day that will be long remembered. We got to Dillard before dark, the air conditioner in our van got hot for a while, But then got alright. And was I glad, because the heat was getting next to me, I was in the time of hot flashes, and very uncomfortable. We decided on a duplex house, we could open it up like a big house and stay two nights. We unloaded our clothes and went out for a nice meal. The porch was so nice and cool. We asked to be seated out there. The ceiling fans were blowing just enough to make the white table clothes blow softly. We decided we might want some coffee before bed time, so after riding through Dillard, finding no store, we went on further and finally saw a place that had some supplies. We needed to have something to put in the refrigerators. We had two so we got some juices, donuts and candy bars, and other snacks. After we got back to the house, we were all pretty pooped. But there was not a silent moment. We snacked and talked and snacked and talked some more. Knowing we would be riding and looking the next day so much we all agreed that we must go to bed. But early the next morning we all were up and ready to go again. My feet started getting tired, but I didn't say anything until some of the others started admitting theirs were too. We had gone down little roads like pig paths to trace down some of mommy Brown's relatives. We found a nephew and his wife which showed us around some in the mountains. They took us by the cemetery where the grandparents were buried. Even though it started raining just before we got there, they got out anyway soon as it slowed some. The day was humid after the rain, but all the dead were visited that day, and tombstones read. We left there and went in some of the antique shops. We saw lots of items that reminded us of days gone by, but didn't care to take any of it home with us. By that time we needed another snack, so we went by the house and cooled off. We had seen the mountain jamboree advertised so after supper we went to the old school auditorium to see the program. We just had to hear some good mountain music and singing before we left. Bobby and I have always liked music and singing. We thoroughly enjoyed the night. It was just good clean fun with some outbursts of laughter. It reminded me of a scripture, that a merry heart does good like a medicine. We enjoyed the "Cloggers." They were the best we had ever seen. As we went back to the house, a heavy fog had settled over, and I was thankful we didn't have far to go, every one was still talking about the events that had happened that day. We sat up late not intending to get up early the next morning. We would get up fairly late and head back home. We stopped to look at the gorges that we had not seen in several years. We had been taking the bypass when going that way, but this day was different, I saw a big pot there, that would go nicely in a sitting room at home, so we bought that and was on our way home. Maybe we will go that way again maybe we won't, until we do, these memories will suffice.

"OUR RECOLLECTIONS OF YESTERYEAR"

We sometimes go from one room to another to get something, and then wonder why we went. But back tracking usually brings the real reason for going. And remembering names is sometimes a problem too, but if we just get busy with other things, out of the blue the name will appear. But when thoughts started coming to us about the old times we had, it seemed like yesterday when they happened and getting the thoughts together for this book was a real joy. Life has been like a vapor, but we have accomplished many things by being here. We have had many valley and mountain top experiences, but the mountain top experiences have always out weighed the valleys. Through the years, Bobby and I have had many stories waiting to be told stored away in our minds just waiting for the right time to share them. We feel like this is the time appointed. Our lives have been simple ones, but we feel mighty blessed! We remember when all the friends and neighbors came to town on Saturday for their weekly supplies, and everybody visited by the side of parked cars until nine o'clock at night when the stores closed. But you didn't try to drive on "Jefferson St" in wet weather, because it was dirt road to the traffic light, and cars would get stuck in the mud.

Ice was made at the "Ice house" and ice creams were five cents a cone at "Rexall" Drug Store. We could take our nicest clothes to "Joe Love" to have cleaned. And you could buy clothes at "Rhodes" store and have them charged. When your shoes got worn, you could take them to "Whites" and have them half-soled. The men could get a twenty five cent hair cut at

"Laniers" barber shop. If the women wanted lots of curls, they could go to "Chick's Beauty Shop" There were five grocery stores, but "Bill White's" was daddy's favorite one. Everything that would be needed to run a household could be purchased in Madison. There were several ten cents stores, but "Armours" really got stocked up around the holidays, and many people used their Lay—Away plan. The stature stood proud in the middle of town, and the "Madison Belmont Hotel" was at the end of south "Main Street." The picture show had good, clean entertainment. You could walk the streets at all times and only find friendly people. The school was in the building now occupied by the cultural center. If you got sick, there were "Doctors" and the "McGeary" hospital if you needed to be hospitalized. And if they couldn't do you any good, there was "Hemperley's" funeral home. If you needed insurance coverage, "W.S. Gardner's" was a good place to get it. If you wanted to live in Madison and didn't have a home, there were two "Boarding" houses that would take care of you. "Pennington Seed and Feed" on south "Main Street" was the place to go when you needed either seed or feed. The two car dealer's "Ben Thompson's Ford" and "Clayton Spears's Dodge and Plymouth" could put you in a brand new car or a super used one. "Ainslie's Drive-In Restaurant" would put you a meal on your car just outside the city. And the main plants that supplied money for many households were the "Thurmond's Sewing plant" and the "International Furniture Company." If you lived in the country, a mail carrier, Mr. Ainslie was always on time and you could mail your packages, get money orders and stamps from him. Mr. Gordan Brewer had a rolling store bus that had a little of everything on it and we would always be glad to see him coming. Just a few of the many conveniences of Madison in the years passed.

PART 4:

"FAMILY PHOTO ALBUM"

Family Photos

1958 Ford Gertrude, Steve and Randy

Steve and Randy Easter

Bobby 1949

Bobby and Airplane

Gertrude

Corine Moon

Gertrude

Gertrude 1st Grade Class

Bobby and Ezra

Bobby, Ezra, Hazel and David

Sons and Daughters of James and Carrie Brown

Bobby and Gertrude's Family

Steve's Graduation

Randy's Graduation

Steve and Randy 1st Picture

Christine, Marjorie, Gertrude and Mary

Gertrude - School Bus

Bobby, Gertrude and Rob at water fountain

Gertrude and Randy Ready for Vacation

Steve & Randy on Donkey

At Daytona Beach

Randy & Steve with Dixie

Wesley, Bobby and Gertrude playing music

Walter Moon

Walter Moon on tractor

Our Parents

Carrie and James Brown

Corine and Walter Moon

About the Author

Gertrude M. Brown has been the secretary of our businesses for over 35 years. She applied and obtained a patent and trademark for a mattress set that her husband invented. Gertrude received a diploma in Interior Design and Decoration in the 1950's. She was born and reared in rural middle Georgia, and she was educated in the Madison school and graduated in 1949. Her hobbies are reading and art painting.

Gertrude is also the author of "Winter Without Shoes"

978-0-595-47056-3
0-595-47056-4

CPSIA information can be obtained
at www.ICGtesting.com
Printed in the USA
FFHW020348281118
49676065-54048FF